# SEEKING SOUND JUDGMENT

*A Memoir*

W. Brian McPherson

Copyright © 2020 W. Brian McPherson
All Rights Reserved

 Year of the Book
135 Glen Avenue
Glen Rock, PA 17327

No part of this publication may be reproduced, distributed, or transmitted in any form or by any means, including photocopying, recording, or other electronic or mechanical methods, without the prior written permission of the publisher, except in the case of brief quotations embodied in critical reviews and certain other noncommercial uses permitted by copyright law.

Print ISBN: 978-1-64649-089-9
Ebook ISBN: 978-1-64649-090-5

# SEEKING SOUND JUDGMENT

# Prologue

*September 1999, Pine Bluff, AR*

"This is it," Makara said as she applied the brakes to her Toyota and pointed to a plain, wood-framed building with the words "Islamic Center & Mosque" displayed in large, embossed letters on the side. I gazed at the roofline. No minarets. One fantasy dashed. A small cupola with a loudspeaker adorned the otherwise residential looking one-story structure. Several bearded, olive-skinned men congregating in front of the mosque noticed me gawking and responded with furrowed brows. I slunk down in my seat.

Makara passed up the empty parking spaces in front of the building and drove through a gate into an unpaved side lot. She pulled past all the cars and parked at the far end, out of sight of the front doors. *People don't sneak into church,* I mused. *But this isn't church*, I reminded myself. I swallowed hard and tried to relax. Thoughts of the vision resurfaced for the third time that day. The vision of the Arabs happened years ago, but remembering it gave me a sense of purpose on my first visit to a mosque.

As we stepped onto the hard packed dirt, the hot, humid air of the early summer evening closed around us. I fought an urge to loosen my tie and take off my suit jacket, but Makara pulled a scarf from her purse and put it on her head.

"It is our custom for women to cover their heads while in the mosque," she explained.

"I understand," I said.

But I didn't understand her distant, apologetic tone and near silence. Makara had barely said a word from the time she picked me up at the motel. What happened to the confident, outgoing person I met on the plane eight weeks earlier? She'd shown enthusiasm when I shared my investigations into the psychology of some of Islam's most venerable tenets and invited me to speak at her mosque. I wanted that person with me.

I tried to center myself in the moment by observing the oak trees that lined the compound. Through the low branches and the chain-link fence beyond them, I could make out small, disheveled houses sitting amid cluttered, unkempt lawns. The palpable abject poverty only heightened a sense of foreboding.

"I asked Dr. Ramejaddin to meet us outside," Makara said as we neared the corner of the building. "He will show you where to go. It is not proper for a woman to accompany a man into the mosque, especially an unmarried woman. Is that okay?"

"Sure, that's fine."

*That explains her solemn mood and discreet arrival. My Egyptian friend needs to avoid appearances of impropriety.* I felt a twinge of guilt, but shook it off. I didn't want to worry about how things looked. I wanted to recapture my confidence. To deliver a cogent speech, I needed self-assurance, not proper appearances.

Dr. Ramejaddin met us at the end of the walkway leading to the mosque. After introducing me, Makara slipped inside, leaving me alone with my host, a tall, trim, professorial-looking man dressed in a dark wool suit and sporting a neatly groomed grey beard. We exchanged pleasantries before he said, "We will be holding a service in the prayer hall first. Then we will move to the social hall for your talk."

We entered the air-conditioned building where about a dozen men congregated in the foyer. Heads turned to watch me, the only Caucasian present. When several returned my nod and smile, I felt my anxiety ease a bit.

We passed through the foyer to a small room that contained a large sink-like trough with a number of spigots.

"The faithful have a tradition of washing hands before a service, as a cleansing ritual," he explained as he performed the task under one of the spigots. I joined him at an adjacent spot. An odd sensation gripped me. It felt as though I was scrubbing for an operation, as though I was about to deliver my speech with the precision of a surgeon. The peculiar impression made me smile.

After we dried our hands we headed to the prayer hall, a spacious meeting room devoid of all furniture except a single chair halfway down on the right side. A waist-high divider cordoned off the left side of the room in the back, enclosing perhaps one fifth of the space.

"We have a chair for you to sit in during prayers," he told me in a hushed tone and gestured toward the seat before leaving me alone.

The room, empty at first, soon filled with men. A mosaic of bold, dark colors and intricate woven patterns filled the hall as each man unfolded his prayer rug onto the plain grey carpet. Some of them threw a sideways glance my way. Every questioning look triggered a nervous smile from me, as I sat with my hands folded in my lap. Finally, the imam walked to the front of the room and rolled out his prayer rug. At this point the women entered en masse through a back entrance into the partitioned area. The rustle of their movement caught my attention, but I suppressed a desire for a backward glance.

The imam offered a number of resonant prayers while the men kneeled on their rugs. Occasionally the congregation gave a response. I saw no printed order of service, yet everyone knew what to say, and when to say it.

The thirty minutes of prayers afforded me plenty of time to think about my peculiar circumstance. As I did, I grew calmer in the reverent atmosphere. I understood that a non-believer rarely attended a service at a mosque, let alone gave the main address at Friday prayers—the most important service of the week—but I felt as though I belonged there. I tapped into a sense of destiny that allayed my apprehensions. *You don't meet a stranger on a plane and get asked to speak at her mosque without the help of fate,* I reasoned. My ideas had captivated my fellow passenger on that forty-minute flight from Memphis to Little Rock. How could a non-believing man elicit such an invitation from an Islamic faithful, a woman at that? I'm sure many in the room would ask that question if they knew the circumstances of how I got there.

After the prayer service concluded, my mind felt clear, as though scrubbed clean by the sounds that echoed in the worship hall during the half-hour service. The men arose in silence and rolled up their prayer rugs as the women filed out the back exit without a word. I sat in silence until Dr. Ramejaddin came to escort me out.

The social hall, with its lower ceiling and smaller floor space, provided a more intimate feeling than the formal setting of the prayer hall. I waited in the front while the men filtered in and took seats on the carpeted floor. The women didn't enter the room, but a group of them gathered just outside the double-door entrance. Their many scarf-covered heads bobbed back and forth as they jockeyed for a good view. Once everyone settled into position, a sense of silent expectancy filled the room. Then Dr. Ramejaddin came to the front and spoke.

"Tonight we are fortunate to have Dr. Brian McPherson here to speak to us. Dr. McPherson is a psychologist who has studied the sounds of human languages and their emotional impact. He has done some fascinating work investigating the sounds we speak and know as the names of Allah that he would like to share with us. Please welcome Dr. McPherson."

The men seated in front of me gave a polite round of applause.

"Thank you for inviting me to speak tonight. It is an honor for me to be here," I said.

"I first became interested in how speech sounds have an emotional impact almost twenty years ago when I attended a yoga retreat that included chanting."

The people almost disappeared as I forgot about the setting and lost myself in the story of how a vision led me to scientific discoveries. I had never related this personal history to my colleagues in psychological research for fear of ridicule, but now the account spilled out with ease and comfort. Comfort, that is, until the front door of the mosque burst open with a crash.

Footsteps striking the tiles in the foyer reverberated in the social hall before a man pushed his way past the women standing in the doorway. I stopped mid-sentence. The latecomer strode halfway toward where I stood before he stopped.

"Why are you listening to this infidel?" The man spoke in a strident voice. "You should not let a Christian infidel speak to you in our place of worship. It is a disgrace to Islam."

# CHAPTER 1

*October 1971, Bethlehem, PA*

The path that led me to a confrontation with a Muslim fundamentalist at the Pine Bluff mosque began almost three decades earlier during my last semester as an undergraduate math major at Lehigh University. Our government's polarizing effort to halt communism in the tiny Southeast Asian country of Vietnam gripped the nation and created countercultural movements on college campuses everywhere, even conservative ones like Lehigh. Protest banners covered walls and marijuana smoke permeated halls.

A slow burning anxiety about the future engulfed me. I could sense the "military industrial complex" exerting a magnetic-like force, pulling me toward its dark, shadowy interior. This monolithic power just needed me to graduate before it would grab me, or rather my mind, and claim it as a slave. It felt useless to struggle against this energy field that had already captured many of my friends. I only had two months of freedom before the "real world" would swallow me like a bat swallows an insect in the dark of night, without any other creature ever knowing or caring. Somewhere in my unconscious, not too far from the surface, I put out a distress signal that pleaded for a way to avoid this depressing fate.

The answer to my subliminal prayer came on an early November day in an unanticipated manner through my best friend, Ray, someone already snared by the web I sought to avoid. He sat beside me in his dress Army uniform on the threadbare couch in my basement apartment and made a pronouncement that jolted me from my path toward what I feared would be a mundane existence of mental slavery and propelled me into an inscrutable future.

"I figure there's about a fifty percent chance that I will commit suicide in the next three weeks." Ray spoke in a flat and distant tone. I looked at my friend with a sinking feeling. His ashen face showed no emotion. The light coming through the high, small windows of the living room shone on his close-cropped blond hair and hunched-over shoulders, giving him a vulnerable look.

My concerns about the future suddenly seemed insignificant in comparison to my friend's, whose statement left me stunned. After a long look at him I felt a sense of urgency. I reached into my pocket, found my car keys, and held them out toward him.

"Here, take these and go."

He looked at me with mistrust and a rueful smile. "You can't be serious. Where would I go?"

"I don't know. Canada. Anywhere. Anywhere is better than going back, if that's how you feel," I said.

He stared at me in silence. For several seconds I returned his gaze, feeling the bond of our friendship. Then he put his head in his hands and sobbed.

Ray's look of disbelief to my proffer of car keys matched one I had seen on him a year earlier. It happened during the nation's first draft lottery at the height of the Vietnam War. The government decided to eliminate student deferments from the draft and make all physically able males eligible for service in the military. They determined the draft order through a random drawing of birthdays. My birthday came in around 200th, high enough that I didn't have to worry about getting selected. Ray didn't fare that well.

When they picked his birthday first, he created a FORTRAN program that printed out a big number '1' on six sheets of computer paper, the kind with the perforated edges, and hung it on his dorm door. Then he scrambled to join the National Guard, at that time a safe way to serve your country without risk of shipping overseas.

His enlistment caused him to postpone his senior year at Lehigh and ship off to Basic Training. On his return from his first weekend pass, his fiancée had given him a ride to the off-campus basement apartment that I shared with two other students. Another person from his Army unit, whose family lived in Bethlehem, planned to pick him up there in a few minutes and take him back to Fort Dix Army Base.

He had told me in short, unemotional statements how he injured his foot in training. It wasn't broken, so the Army kept him in training. But the injury made him lag behind others. That brought down the wrath of his drill sergeant. The drill sergeant kept riding him. He didn't think he could take it much longer. Then came the suicide statement.

After a minute or so his sobs subsided and I laid my hand on his shoulder. "It's all right," I told him. I sat beside him in stillness just breathing the moldy air of the dungeon-like apartment, not knowing what else to say or do.

Finally, he took a deep breath. "You know, it makes me feel better just to know that you would do that for me... just to know that you care enough to do something like that."

I didn't say anything, but just looked at him with a feeling of compassion.

After a few moments he took another deep breath and squared his sturdy frame. "You know, I think I'm going to be all right now."

"Good," I said. "But if you need anything... I mean, if you need anything at all, man, call me. I'll come over to the base and give you a ride, or do whatever I have to. I mean it." Fort Dix was a couple of hours from campus.

"Okay. Thanks, man," he said in a relieved tone. He looked pensive for a moment and then asked, "Do you have a piece of paper and pen? I want to write a letter to Kris."

I got up and found one of my notebooks, tore a sheet out of it, and handed it to him, along with a pen.

"I just said goodbye to her, and at the time I felt like I really didn't care if I saw her again. I just wasn't feeling anything. I need to tell her I love her, and that I'm going to be all right."

As he wrote I pulled a Dave Van Ronk album from my record collection and put it on the turntable. A raspy voice singing about a wandering wombat gave the room an irreverent buzz and helped diffuse the tension.

After a few minutes of concentration and writing Ray folded up the letter.

"Okay. I needed to get that down," he said. He paused a few seconds before continuing. "I really want her to get this. I wonder how I should do that."

There was a short pause before what he said sank in. "No problem, man," I told him. "I can give it to her in person tonight." I felt an urge to demonstrate the sincerity of my offer to help, and didn't consider the two-and-one-half hour drive, one-way, an obstacle.

He thanked me, and then we sat and talked about the music until a horn beeped outside. I walked with him to the car that was taking him back to Basic Training and said goodbye.

Ray's distress hit me on a personal level. We'd spent great times together in the past two years, and I felt closer to him than anyone else. I wanted to do whatever I could to help him. With a sense of duty I drove the one hundred and twenty miles to York to deliver the letter to his fiancée, Kris. When I returned after nine that evening, I couldn't get my mind focused on studying for the next day's test. I went to bed without studying, tossing and turning for a long period before falling asleep. The next morning when I sat down to cram for the eleven o'clock exam I still couldn't get my mind away from the events of the previous day.

When I realized that I wouldn't be able to concentrate on the high level math test that I hadn't studied for, I left to visit my fiancée, Meryl, to find some comfort. She went to school in Indiana, PA, over five hours away. The self-assured, confident person I had portrayed to my friend didn't seem so self-assured or confident in the aftermath.

# CHAPTER 2

*December 1971, Eastern and Central PA*

Ray's voice sounded upbeat. "I got a pass for the weekend, man. Any way you can get me a ride to York?"

It was six weeks after my friend's emotional suicidal breakdown and almost the end of my semester. I thought for a moment of all the reading I needed to do and the short time available to do it, but soon put the thought out of mind as I recalled Ray's previous gloomy outlook and my promise to help.

"Yeah, no problem. I'd be glad to do it. Just tell me how to find you."

I picked him up and we drove to his fiancée's home. Then the three of us drove to Kirk and Jeri's. Kirk was a sculptor who lived just down the road from Ray's folks. Jeri was Kirk's wife. Ray wanted me to meet Kirk who, according to Ray, had a "mind like an encyclopedia and can talk forever about anything."

As we pulled into the driveway an energetic wolfhound with long, wavy red and white fur greeted us and dashed around our car. Her lack of a growl or even a bark and her wagging tail signaled her friendship. A twenty-something man of medium stature sporting a bushy red beard and shaggy thick hair came to the back door of the old farmhouse as we got out of the car. His appearance from the long hair on his head to the moccasins on his feet spoke "Hippie."

After introductions, Kirk led us into an anteroom where we hung our coats. When we entered the living area a four-foot-tall wooden statue greeted us.

"Hey, there's Gimli," I said pointing to the figure that resembled how my mind's eye had pictured Tolkien's dwarf.

Kirk raised his eyebrows, "Ah, you recognize him."

I leaned over to inspect the carving. "Nice," I said, as I ran my fingers over the grooves in the creature's coat. "What kind of wood?"

"Cherry."

I continued to caress the piece. "How did you get all of those details?"

Kirk cocked his head to one side. "Do you want to see my studio? I can show you my setup with all my tools."

"Sure."

We walked through the room and to a stairwell that led down into the basement where Kirk kept a well-lit workbench and several racks of sculpting tools. On one end of the bench a large vice held a piece of soapstone which had the rough shape of a pipe.

Kirk picked up tool after tool and talked about each of their unique characteristics and uses. From the tools he delved into his creations, pieces he'd finished, works in progress, those he planned to do, where he got the stones, how he intended to use them. He threw in comments about what particular artist influenced several works in progress lying on the floor, and how his work differed. Neither Ray nor I needed to ask questions after that first rhetorical one. He mesmerized us with an exhaustive account of the art of stone sculpture.

When we got that glazed-over look, Kirk realized he had exceeded our capacity for retaining details. We returned to the living room on the first floor and sat down on the large, soft floor cushions that Kirk used as his main furniture.

"Have you read Carlos Castaneda's book *A Separate Reality* yet?" Ray asked Kirk.

"Yes, I've been digging it."

"What do you think about the idea of the reality of the sorcerer's world being different from the reality that we perceive?" I asked both of them. Castaneda's work fascinated me, too.

"I think that Huxley explains that pretty well in his book *Doors of Perception*," Kirk said.

"Oh?" I hadn't read Huxley's book, but I tried not to let it show.

"Yeah, Huxley says that the way we perceive the world is limited by the way we filter our perceptions. If we could just learn how to let things pass through our natural filters we could see a whole new reality."

"Oh, so you think the sorcerers in Don Juan's world have learned how to perceive things that normal people filter out, like the 'lines of the world'?"

"Yeah, I'd say you've pretty much got it."

"So what about when Castaneda talked about floating around in a bubble?" Ray added a new twist from a bizarre section of Castaneda's book.

Kirk laughed at the image created by Ray's question, but before he could add anything we heard a vehicle pull up outside. We got up to see the new arrival. Kirk opened the door and the hound bounded out to welcome Eric, a tall, muscular psychologist friend and patron of Kirk's, a man blessed with Scandinavian good looks and the confidence a person gains after two graduate degrees from an Ivy League school.

After introductions Kirk took out one of the pipes he had carved from soapstone and filled it with marijuana. He lit it, took a toke, and passed it to Ray. While we took turns with the pipe, Eric and Kirk talked about Kirk's latest work, a stunning piece of black marble that resembled an Egyptian queen. Eric had commissioned the work and came to pick it up. He'd already paid for it, or rather bartered for it, with Ruby, Kirk's wolfhound. Eric bred registered borzoi. Kirk chose the only red-coated one Eric ever raised.

When the last bit of smoke escaped the bowl, Eric went out to his VW bus and brought back a large reel-to-reel tape player, the size of a small suitcase.

"A friend of a friend from Columbia University gave me this tape," he said as he threaded the magnetic tape from one reel through the tape head and onto the empty reel. "I want you to hear it. It is some far out stuff." Eric hit play.

We listened to the story of how Richard Alpert became transformed into Baba Ram Dass. I found the backstory riveting. A psychology professor, kicked out of Harvard for use and promotion of LSD, struggles and searches for truth. He winds up in India and undergoes a transformation to Baba Ram Dass, a spiritual leader.

The most memorable part of the evening occurred when a voice on the tape started a question, "Do you remember the time that we..." but before the whole question got stated it was interrupted by, "Don't think about the past, just be here now."

Another question started, "How long do you think we will..." and another interruption, "Don't think about the future, just be here now. If you can truly 'be here now', then all your cares will go away."

As we listened Kirk filled another bowl and took a deep toke from the pipe and passed it on to me. Nothing like a little marijuana to make advice from a tape seem like an answer for all of your problems. I took a hit and passed the pipe on.

After the forty-five-minute tape finished, I wanted to know the others' thoughts on a crucial element of the story. On the night the former Harvard professor arrived at the ashram, his future guru stunned him with a show of clairvoyance. The psychologist had been thinking about his mother's death when the holy man perceived this without being told. Further, the guru correctly identified the cause of her death—spleen cancer—a fact Alpert had shared with nobody at the ashram. At this point Alpert broke down. It was the decisive point in his transformation.

"How do you think the guru knew about his mother?" I asked the group.

"Drugs," Kirk said in a matter-of-fact manner.

"What do you mean?" I asked. "Drugs to give the guru power to read Ram Dass's mind?"

"No," Kirk replied, "remember? Ram Dass said the folks at the ashram fed them just before that happened."

"Yeah, but..." I hesitated. "How would drugging Ram Dass give the guru that ability?" Kirk had just taken a big toke and was holding his breath. When he didn't answer after a few seconds, I answered my own question. "So you think he remembered the story wrong." I shrugged my shoulders and shook my head. "I guess he could just as easily have made the whole thing up," I said, feeling deflated. I'd wanted to believe the guru had special powers.

"What do you think about his comment on the astral plane?" I asked. "That just a drug illusion, too?" Ram Dass had talked about his "visits" to the astral plane; he insisted that it existed and was just as real as this plane of existence.

Kirk's eyes opened wide and he raised his eyebrows. "Do you know?" he said, turning the question back to me, and also messing with my mind by repeating a phrase used by Ram Dass. Ram Dass said he and others constantly looked into the eyes of people they met while on their spiritual quest and asked, "Do you know?" because they all wanted to find a teacher who "knew."

"I don't know," I admitted. "I guess I'm skeptical. I think he believes what he said, but I guess I'd want more evidence." Part of me wanted to sound sophisticated and not swept up by the allure of Ram Dass. However, Ram Dass's story of how he found a teacher for raja yoga captured my pot-fueled imagination. Raja yoga differed from the yoga that I knew, the yoga of postures or asanas done for physical benefit. Ram Dass told how raja yoga cultivated the mind through meditation and other practices with the aim of liberation from the ego.

Ram Dass's description of raja yoga and his experiences on the astral plane made it sound like an enchanting trip. I had heard of the astral plane, but thought it only existed in the imagination of folks of certain Eastern religions and that it was their equivalent of heaven, a place to go when you died. But Ram Dass's story replaced that stale notion with something enticing. Was there a separate reality that one could enter by leaving the physical body? And then you would return to your body? The path lying before me, a career as a mathematician, seemed void of purpose and fulfillment in comparison to Ram Dass's world.

"But, if it was drug induced, then why haven't I had the same kind of trips?" Kirk cocked his head and grinned. "I just sit here and get stoned, and don't go anywhere."

"Do you think that when Castaneda talked about floating, as if in a bubble, he was doing that in astral form, or just describing a drug-induced state?" Ray asked, getting back to the question he had posed just prior to Eric's arrival.

"He was definitely on drugs," Kirk answered. "He even wrote about the peyote. He…"

"Aw, it was all made up," Eric interjected. "Pure fiction. *Steppenwolf* meets the southwest."

From Baba Ram Dass to Castaneda to a Herman Hesse novel in a minute is enough to make any head spin, but if your mind is already spinning on pot it just seems natural. "Speaking of Hesse," I said, "I just finished *The Glass Bead Game*." The works of Hesse had gained a vast following in the counterculture of the '60s and early '70s. Eric's mention of *Steppenwolf*, one of Hesse's most popular books with the counterculture at that time because of its explicit depiction of drug use, hit one of my buttons.

"Ah, *Magister Ludi*," Eric responded with the alternate title to *The Glass Bead Game*. "I really felt let down by the ending."

In the novel the main character, the master, is part of an elite order whose members devote their lives to intellectual pursuits. As the story progresses, the master begins to find these pursuits meaningless and leaves the order. In the end, the main character dives into a lake with a young student and drowns.

"Oh, not me. That was my favorite Hesse."

"But when the magister dies at the end it left me really bummed out," he complained.

"Because you identified with the master," I said, not asking, just observing.

"Yes, of course," Eric confirmed. "Didn't you?"

"No. I was the student with him. The master was Hesse."

"Really?" he asked. "How did you come up with that?"

"In the master's circular petition to leave the order, I felt as though Hesse was actually addressing the reader. It was like he was telling the reader he was leaving. You know it was his last work."

"Interesting," Eric replied.

"So from that point, I read it as though the main character was Hesse speaking. When he took on the young student after he left the order, that was me. I kept that interpretation through the rest of the novel. When the master died and the student remained it had a profound effect on me. It was like a mystical experience, as if I received the knowledge and blessing of Hesse when he left this existence and passed on to the unknown."

Until that point Eric and I hadn't said much to each other. Perhaps the gap between our ages had created a barrier, but our common interest in Hesse knocked down such obstacles.

"That's a far better interpretation than I had," Eric said, acknowledging my analytical ability.

While Eric and I discussed Hesse, Kirk got out his guitar and tuned it.

"Are you going to play us one of your drones?" his wife asked, sounding hopeful. "You've been making some interesting music lately, very Eastern sounding."

Kirk didn't say anything but started to play an open-tuned number that had a drone-like quality that kept a steady meter using a common base chord while floating a melody above. Everyone quit their conversations and listened.

After a few minutes Kirk stopped. As people expressed appreciation for his playing I held out my hand toward Kirk's guitar. "Can I give it a try?"

"Sure." Kirk handed me the instrument.

I re-tuned it to standard guitar pitches. Although I'd performed with a rock band in high school and knew many tunes, I didn't consciously try to play anything but just let the notes flow as I felt them. An eerie, atonal tune devoid of meter emerged, reflecting my spaced-out, mystical mood. I finished with long pauses between the last few notes.

When I finally put my picking hand down, several seconds after my last note, Eric commented. "Wow! That was hypnotic. It got to be like I could anticipate what the next note was going to be and when you were going to play it."

"But it was so random!" Jeri interjected, not hiding her critical opinion of the piece. "How could you anticipate anything?"

"I know, but it was like it was pulling me along. Like I was there—a part of it, and I just knew what was going to happen."

Eric's comment brought my awareness back to the room. I struggled to focus for a second, then got up, handed the guitar back to Kirk, and headed toward the back door. "I need to grab some fresh air."

Eric put his tapes back into cases and closed the lid on his machine. "I'm going to take this back to my van."

Outside I inhaled several deep breaths of the cool air, allowing its calming effect to bring my mind back to earth, back from the soaring place the music had taken me.

After Eric put his equipment away he walked over to where I stood. "Kirk says you will graduate this semester."

"Yes, that's right, I guess," I replied without enthusiasm.

"Do you have any plans?" Eric seemed to be going somewhere with the question.

I raised an eyebrow, as if to say, "Why do you ask?" Then I said, "Nothing immediate. I guess I'll start looking for a job. I'm graduating a semester early, so I have a couple of months before the rest of my class hits the job market."

"Well, I'm looking for someone to live in my cabin for insurance purposes. I have a little bungalow sitting on twenty-eight acres about thirty miles southeast of Clarion University where I used to teach. Someone had been living there, but she left. So if I want to keep my insurance low, I need someone to move in. It's not very fancy. No running water, but it does have a phone, electricity, and a gas fireplace."

I nodded, but didn't reply. I hadn't thought too much about what I would do in January after the end of this semester. I figured I would have to move back in with my parents.

"Rent free," Eric added when I was silent. "I could even help buy food supplies. I would come up on weekends. I live and work in Maryland, but I am trying to develop the property. Eventually I would like to make the place self-sufficient, where I could make a living by breeding my dogs and growing my own food. My ultimate goal is to make a community for like-minded people to live, work, and play together."

"Interesting," I said. My head started to fill with a fantasy. The "Back to the Land" movement of the late '60s and early '70s had recently caught my attention. The *Mother Earth News* had inspired me and made me long for a chance to live a simpler life. I didn't have any land to live on, but the allure of "living off the land" had me wishing for such an opportunity, and now it seemed that it had appeared, a life raft from nowhere. How could I not take up Eric's offer? Although I had only met him that evening, we seemed to have some common interests, and he had provided enough flattery that I felt relaxed and not threatened by him. "Well, my finals aren't over until January 13th, but after that I would be interested."

"I have no problem waiting a month."

"Then we have a deal."

I felt that at worst I had just agreed to a Thoreau vacation in the woods, but maybe I had just started on a journey toward a better life.

Eric gave me his phone number, and I agreed to get in touch when my finals were over.

# Chapter 3

*December 1971, Bethlehem, PA*

After returning to school the next day, I found it difficult to study. Thoughts of living self-sufficiently kept interfering. I remembered Ram Dass's advice that if you can truly "be here now," then all your problems will disappear. I wanted the problems with my studies to go away, so I checked out a book on Zen Buddhism from the library and tried to meditate. Until the day before, mysticism just seemed like another fad of popular culture started by the Beatles, but now it looked like a path toward a sensible, spiritual way of life.

I assumed a lotus pose in the middle of the living room and tried to exorcise thoughts about living on the land, schoolwork, and other distractions. As I attempted to meditate, memories about my past spirituality, or rather lack thereof, crept into my consciousness. I remembered taking Catechism class when I turned twelve years old and joining my mother's Methodist church, not because I wanted to, but because my mother forced me. I only went through the motions.

Although she was devout, my father had nothing to do with religion. He might have been agnostic or even an atheist. I don't know. He never bothered to tell me the philosophical reason why he preferred to play tennis on Sunday mornings rather than "warble with the Christians," as he put it. His eschewing of church had made it easy for me as a teenager to demand my own religious freedom, or rather freedom from religion. I spent most Sunday mornings in bed catching up on sleep.

As I tried to reconcile my past lack of faith with my sudden plunge into Eastern spirituality, a repressed memory from early childhood flashed to mind. I remembered an experience from when I was five years old. In my mind I could see the house where I lived. My bedroom had two doors, one leading into my parents' bedroom and one leading to the hallway in the back of the house. I could still see that dark, foreboding hallway that accessed a seldom used bathroom, a musty workroom, and a narrow stairway that led down to the first floor.

Several times I had told my mom that the back door scared me, but she always assured me there was nothing to be afraid of and gave me a kiss. Then she'd ask me to say my prayer. "Now I lay me down to sleep. I pray the Lord my soul to keep. If I should die before I wake, I pray the Lord my soul to take. Five little angels around my bed, one at the foot, one at the head, one to sing, and one to pray, and one to take my soul away."

This "if I should die" part bothered me. How was I going to die? Even at that young age I understood that old people could die in their sleep, but not young boys like me. I knew that the only way a young person might die was from some terrible disease like polio, or by doing something reckless, like riding a bike into traffic or falling out of a tree. Since I wasn't sick, I figured the only way I could "die before I wake" was if some bad man came up the back stairs and through the back bedroom door while I slept, and killed me.

I became fixated on the back door to the point that each night, after my mother left, I would stare at it, almost shaking in the bed. One night, while obsessing over the menacing door, I thought about those five angels and whether they possessed power to keep bad guys from coming up the back steps and attacking me. I stared at the door, as usual, but this time without fear. Instead I tried to invoke the protection of my angels. After an intense effort of concentration a bright light in the shape of a face appeared above the door.

The glow of the image filled me with both a feeling of safety and one of foreboding. Nobody ever told me that you could see angels. In fact, my mother told me it wasn't possible. So if I couldn't see angels, what did I see? Did I just imagine this bright radiance?

After seeing this vision I never worried about the back steps again. In fact, from then on I avoided looking at the door that led to those steps so that I wouldn't think about seeing or imagining angels. I knew I did enough bad things, like sneaking cookies and starting fights with my neighbor. I wanted to avoid contact in case the angel would confront me about those transgressions. My strategy was to let them focus on their job and not draw too much attention to myself, so I'd suppressed this memory until now.

As a child, steering clear of angels made more sense to me than embracing them, but with my newfound interest in things of the spirit, my perspective changed. Had I seen a manifestation from the astral plane that evening as a five year old? Was this connected to what Ram Dass talked about? As I sat reminiscing over my past vision I felt a desire to experience the astral plane, to embrace the spirit or whatever I'd seen on that long ago night. It seemed much more vital than studying the mundane, spiritless world of math.

Ram Dass said he felt that when he taught at Harvard he really didn't know the subject of psychology, his specialty, and he feared that he would spend the next forty years feeling that way. I felt like I was headed for a similar trap. Even if I knew my subject, I didn't really like it that much. I majored in math only because I did well in it, earning the highest grades in high school, and the highest SAT scores. Doing well in something doesn't equate to enjoying it, but a day ago I hadn't seen any choice, other than pursuing what I could do. Now a real choice stood before me. I could plod on deeper into what I considered a tedious world or follow a dream.

I sat on the couch in my apartment with my legs crossed and just smiled, instead of studying for finals. I didn't finish my work that semester and left school nine credits short of graduation. Afterward I headed to Eric's cabin where I could meditate without worrying about studying.

# Chapter 4

*June 1972, Northwestern PA*

With a small, metal scoop I moved the hot coals from the grill into the fire pit, then grabbed a handful of kindling and threw it on top of the coals. Wisps of smoke escaped through crevasses in the pile of dried pine branches. I took off my t-shirt and used it to fan the coals with animated strokes until a flame burst through the twigs. I added several larger sticks and fanned some more. Before long, fire filled the ring and cast dancing shadows on the cabin wall. It lit the dimming twilight and radiated enough heat that I didn't need to put the shirt back on to ward off the chill from the falling temperatures of the June evening.

I lay back on the soft pillow that cushioned the wooden deck chair and closed my eyes. An image of small, gray stones appeared, an impression etched into my visual cortex as a result of moving crushed limestone all day. In the morning a big tri-axle dump truck deposited six tons of grade 2-B gravel at the end of the driveway. We spread the load with just a couple of shovels, a metal rake, and a wheelbarrow. I could feel my aching muscles complaining about the job.

Every weekend since spring weather made outside work feasible, Eric drove the five hours from Baltimore to join me at the cabin. We worked together on taming his twenty-eight acres, although it still remained a very rough patch of land, a wild territory with an ironic twist. The attractive natural setting of woods, fields, and stream bordered an interstate highway. Fortunately a stand of pines obscured the traffic from the cabin, which sat about one hundred yards from the road, although the whine of truck tires on pavement penetrated the dense branches with enough intensity to keep me from mistaking the setting for an isolated retreat.

A mountain stream cut the property into two pieces, eight acres on the side with the cabin, and twenty acres of woods on the other side, inaccessible by road. Before they built the interstate you could drive across the stream via a sturdy wooden bridge. However, the highway construction crew rerouted the water so that the old bridge now went over a dry stream bed. The new route of the water, a straight v-cut channel west of the old creek bed, ran seventy-five feet below the concrete pillars that supported the interstate traffic. With nothing but low brush growing along the banks of angular rocks, the new channel had a sterile feeling. In contrast, the old, meandering trail that the stream once took now gave the appearance of a museum, housing masterful works of rounded rock sculptures, interspersed with oak and maple saplings, all shaded by majestic hemlock trees.

The three-room cabin sat in the middle of four acres of woods on a hill above the creek. The construction of the highway left the four-acre field below the cabin a wasteland. It resembled a reclaimed strip mine like those found in that area of Pennsylvania, a moonscape of rocks where nothing could grow except some scrubby looking pine trees.

*It's not paradise*, I told myself, when I first came five months earlier. A bit of an understatement, considering that in addition to much of the land looking like it had been raped, I didn't have running water in the cabin. I used an outhouse for a toilet, and I took baths in a very cold stream. But I was willing to put up with the inconveniences for the dream of living off the land that it harbored.

*Honk! Honk!*

I opened my eyes and looked at Eric. "That sounds like it's coming from the gate," I said. The gate at the edge of the property was about two hundred yards away.

"I bet I know what it's about," Eric said, getting up from his seat and putting his plate on the picnic table. "Some locals paid a visit last night. They arrived at the same time as I did. They told me they were looking for the nudist camp."

"The nudist camp?"

"Yeah, a couple of weekends ago after you finished washing at the stream and left for the cabin, two guys with fishing gear came walking down the other side of the creek. I was still naked, just taking my time finishing my bath when they appeared. I stood there drying myself off, not hurrying to get dressed. I didn't care if they saw me." He opened the back door, reached around the corner, and grabbed a shotgun, one he had borrowed from our neighbor earlier that day.

As Eric walked down the driveway he left his words trailing behind him. "I told them it was my land and they were trespassing. They left without talking. I'm guessing they started the story about the nudist camp."

I called after him. "So what are you going to do?"

"Scare them off." He didn't look back as he headed down the steep section of the road. "This time for good."

"So that's why you got the gun," I said in a low voice that Eric didn't hear.

I shook my head as I stood and picked up the used paper plates and threw them into the flames. I watched them catch fire and then closed the bag of chips and took them and the ketchup inside where I sat down with a book. In the next few minutes shotgun blasts twice interrupted my attempts to escape into another world.

About ten minutes after he left, Eric came in, out of breath. He put the gun back in the corner before sitting down next to me with a grin on his face.

"So what happened?" I asked.

"I doubt they'll be back," he said, his chest still heaving from running.

I raised my eyebrows but didn't say anything.

"There were about five or six of them. Instead of coming up the road, they had crossed the field to the creek. I saw their heads poking above the top of the bank as they snuck along the edge of the water, so I hunkered down behind the big oak where the road turns, and waited. They got to where the creek comes closest to the road before they climbed the bank and headed in my direction. When they were about twenty yards away I stepped out and fired a shot over their heads."

Eric let out a big laugh as he leaned forward and slapped his knee. "You should have seen them run. Every which way. Some back along the creek. Some down the road. I ran down the road after two of them and fired another shot as they reached the gate where two cars were parked. They got into the second car and took off. I ran up to the other car, and..." he paused as he reached into his back pocket and took out a leather sheath. With a grin he pulled out a large hunting knife and held it up.

"It felt so good when I sunk this into each of those front tires."

I gave a slight shrug and turned back to my book. My eyes followed the words on the page, but my mind didn't register their meanings. I wanted to believe that Eric had just told me about a mundane everyday experience, but the after effects of the image he just painted made me feel as though something had grabbed my intestines and started twisting.

Eric got up and poured himself a glass of water from the pitcher in the refrigerator before coming back in the room and sitting again.

"After I slit the tires, I waited in the woods above the gate, about halfway up the side of the hill. In another couple of minutes I saw several others coming up from the creek along the fence row. They hopped into the car and slammed it into reverse. *Whoo!* They hit the gas so hard they tore up a big patch of dirt." Eric took a big drink of water.

"It would have been funny if they'd had front-wheel drive." He laughed out loud and then put down his glass and stood up.

"I'm going to go hang out in the woods above the gate," he said. He walked back into the kitchen and picked up the shotgun. "I'm guessing those guys won't be too happy when they discover the flat tires. I don't know if they might want to get some revenge."

"Why don't you just call the cops?"

"Well, if they come back..." he didn't finish his statement before he went out the door.

The rest of the night proved uneventful. Perhaps the trespassers had enough. I knew I had my fill, even at the distance from which I participated.

The next day Eric left before noon. Just after I sat down at the picnic table to eat lunch, I got a call on the cabin's phone. It was the neighbor who lived just before the gate.

"Two men are down here at my place and want to know if it is okay for them to come up and pay a visit," he told me.

"Yeah, it's okay," I said, without thinking about asking who they were or what they wanted. Weeks at the cabin without any contact from anyone except Eric on the weekends made the thought of visitors attractive, but after I hung up the phone thoughts of the previous night came back to me. Nobody ever visited me at the cabin before, so reason told me that today's guests had something to do with last night's episode. The thought of an encounter with two angry men brought back the tight feeling in my gut and a surge of adrenaline. I hurried outside and headed to the dog kennel.

Eric housed two of his borzoi breeding stock on the grounds of the cabin to keep me company and to give the rest of his dogs in his main kennel in Maryland more room. A borzoi, or Russian wolfhound, as a rule doesn't show aggression to humans, but not everyone knows that and their impressive size and athletic body can be imposing. Both dogs got up when I jogged over to the gate. Caesar, a twelve-year-old male, walked as if in slow motion over to the food dish. Gertie, a three-year-old female, stretched before prancing in front of me in anticipation of a chance to run. Although bigger and more intimidating, I didn't trust Caesar enough to let him out ever since he had run away for over a day one time. I knew Gertie would listen to me. When I let her out she ran two wide circles around the pen at top speed before following me over to the picnic table, where she lay at my feet as I went back to eating lunch.

When two men dressed in blue jeans and t-shirts walked up the lane two minutes later, Gertie ran to greet them. She got three-quarters of the way to them before they stopped in their tracks. I smiled when I saw them hesitate, and then called the dog back to my side. Once she sat down I motioned to the visitors to join me. The two walked up to the edge of the concrete slab that served as the cabin's deck. They looked to be around twenty years old. The taller, thinner one had a pack of cigarettes rolled up in his shirt sleeve, exposing his larger than average biceps. The shorter one had a baseball hat on backwards and stood with his hands on his hips with his weight shifted onto one leg. Their glares did not speak friendship.

"Afternoon, guys. What can I do for you?" I greeted them with a smile, but did not get up from my seat or even put down my soup spoon. They did not return my smile.

"This your place?" the taller one asked.

"No. I do live here, but I'm just the caretaker, not the owner." I avoided their piercing glares by looking at my food.

"You here last night?"

I poked at the last bit of chili in my bowl, like I was looking for a piece of courage, before looking up and replying, "Yeah, I was."

"Did you hear some shots last night?" The question came from the shorter, stockier fellow.

"Yes, I did. Eric, the guy who owns this place, told me he fired warning shots at some people he caught trespassing."

The shorter man crossed his arms on his chest. "He told you, huh? You weren't there?" It sounded like a challenge.

"No. I stayed up here in the cabin. I was reading a book while it happened," I said, scraping the remaining chili onto my spoon and trying to keep my nerves steady.

The taller one also put his hands on his hips, tilted his head to one side, and used a confronting tone. "Where's this Eric guy now?"

I looked the tall dude in the eye and let my voice hover somewhere between cocky and patronizing, not a good recipe to win a friend, but a great smokescreen to cover up fear. "He left for Maryland about an hour ago. He lives and works down there. He comes up here some weekends."

Finally, the tall one issued the ultimatum he had come to deliver. "Well, someone slit two of my tires last night and I aim to make them pay for it."

Gertie raised her head in response to the man's tone. A growl might have served me better, but at least she noticed the tension.

"I don't know nothing about no tires," I said in an even tone, as I focused on spooning the last bit of my lunch into my mouth.

The two men scowled but remained silent while I chewed.

When I finished the bite, I said, "Sorry I can't help you fellows out. Maybe you could come back on a Saturday. That's your best bet on catching Eric here." I held back a smile. I didn't need to overdo the patronizing.

With looks of disdain and a slight snort from the taller man, the two turned around and walked back down the lane.

Eric called me Friday morning to tell me he planned on arriving that night. I fed the dogs and left.

# Chapter 5

*July 1972, Southcentral PA*

From the cabin I drove straight to Kirk's place. Kirk and Jeri had visited the cabin while I lived there, and Kirk and I shared the dream of living there in a commune of sorts. I wanted to relate my reason for leaving before Eric reported to them that I'd abandoned the place.

When I arrived Kirk was in his backyard working on a large piece of pink alabaster. As I got out of my car Ruby greeted me with her tail wagging.

"Hey, so you came to visit *us* this time," Kirk said in a loud voice as he put down his hammer and chisel.

"I've left the cabin for good." My serious tone revealed my troubled state.

Kirk did a double take at my abrupt greeting and motioned toward me. "Come on in. Let's talk."

We went inside and I told him the story about Eric's response to the intruders and their return visit. "I couldn't stay there with that kind of karma floating around."

"I don't blame you. I guess we were kind of naïve thinking we could create a community there. I knew there'd always be issues when one person is the landowner. It's never really communal then. That person has final say over everything. And when that person is not centered in the spirit, you're gonna have problems."

"Thanks for understanding," I said. I got up from the kitchen table. "Enough about the cabin. Tell me, what have you carved lately?"

He spent the next half hour showing me his latest creations until Ray and Kris arrived. Ray had survived his stint in Basic and had just returned from his two weeks of summer service. He looked tanned and relaxed, all ready to go back to Lehigh for his final year. He and Kris planned on moving to Bethlehem where Kris was to start a new job as a counselor. They had stopped by to tell Kirk and Jeri about Kris's job.

Jeri invited us all to stay for supper and we worked together picking corn from the garden, firing up the grill for the burgers, and getting everything ready for a feast celebrating Kris's new job and Ray's return to Lehigh. Following the meal we relaxed in the living room and shared a ceremonial pipe. After the bowl burned out Kirk grabbed his guitar from the corner and began to tune it. While adjusting one of the strings it broke with a loud twang.

The strange noise caused everyone to stop talking. Kirk put his hand on his beard and held it there for several seconds, staring at the broken string before putting the instrument down.

"I'm going to throw the *I Ching*," he said.

I knew of Kirk's practice of consulting the *I Ching* at critical or significant times. Kirk took the broken string as an omen.

I'd first learned about the *I Ching*—an ancient Chinese divination system—when Hesse incorporated it into his book's eponymous glass bead game. After learning that the *I Ching* was considered one of the most important books in the entire history of Chinese civilization, I bought a copy of a popular translation which detailed how to use three coins as a system for divining answers to questions or understanding situations faced in life.

During my stay at the cabin, the *I Ching* had been the only book that I studied. I spent many long evenings poring over each of the sixty-four patterns and their detailed interpretations. I knew the names and at least some level of interpretation of many. I developed a deep respect, a reverent awe, of the *I Ching*. It always seemed to ring true on the occasions when I used it to help me understand a particular problem nagging me. Was I just fooling myself into believing that throwing coins could portend the future? It didn't seem possible from a Western perspective, but from my fresh Eastern viewpoint I didn't rationalize about it. I just experienced it.

Kirk returned from his study where he stored his divination coins and his copy of the *I Ching*. He handed the book to his wife and sat down on a cushion on the floor. Each time he threw the coins, they came up two tails and one head, the combination signifying a young yang, or unbroken line. No one needed to look up the name of the hexagram associated with six yang lines. An all yang series corresponded to the first hexagram, called the Creative, and meant the presence of a strong creative force, apropos for an artist.

"That's the fourth time I threw 'The Creative' this week."

"You really have sculpted some great new pieces lately," Jeri said with a nod.

Kirk's result seemed undramatic. We all recognized the high level of creativity in his work.

"That's like preaching to the choir, man," Ray said with a laugh, and then added, "Maybe the omen wasn't for you." He put his hand out toward Kirk. "Here, let me cast. Today feels like an important day for me."

Ray's sequence went yang-yang-yang, then yin-yin-yin.

Jeri started reading from the book.

"Standstill. Also called Stagnation. Heaven and earth are out of communion and all things are benumbed. What is above has no relation to what is below, and on earth confusion and disorder prevail. The dark power is within, the light power is without. Weakness is within, harshness without. Within are the inferior, and without are the superior. The way of inferior people is in ascent—"

This ominous sounding explanation of Ray's cast created a palpable tension in the air. Something didn't seem right. Ray's going back to school shouldn't portend weakness and stagnation.

"Wait," I interrupted. Details from the hours of studying the book came back to me in a rush. "Stagnation is three yin and then three yang. He threw the three yang first, then the yin. That combination is called Peace. It comes right before Stagnation in the book."

Jeri looked again at the sequence she had written down for Ray's cast and then at the book. "Oh, wow! You're right. I was reading the wrong one. I'm so sorry. I'm really glad you caught that."

She began to read from the book again. "Peace. The small departs. The great approaches. Good fortune. Success."

I could hear an audible sigh from Ray.

Jeri continued, "This hexagram denotes a time in nature when heaven seems to be on earth. Heaven has placed itself beneath the earth, and so their powers unite in deep harmony. Then peace and blessing descend upon all living things. In the world of man it is a time of social harmony. Inside, at the center, in the key position, is the light principle; the dark principle is outside. Thus the light has a powerful influence, while the dark is submissive. In this way each receives its due. When the good elements of society occupy a central position and are in control, the evil elements come under their influence and change for the better."

"That's a big difference, peace instead of stagnation," Ray said with a relieved laugh. "How did you know that she picked the wrong one?" he asked me.

"I studied the book many hours these past six months."

Ray shook his head, and then with a sideways look of amazement said, "I just realized I've been playing the glass bead game with the master these past couple of years."

In truth we had never played the glass bead game. In fact, no one has ever played the game because it is only a game in the imagination of Hesse and his readers, but we had both read and discussed Hesse's book before and we knew that the master of the game had a keen intellect with the ability to synthesize disciplines. Young guys, as a rule, don't have a penchant for paying compliments to one another, especially such personal and abstract ones as I perceived this to be. I felt a wave of emotion as silence penetrated the room.

After a few seconds Jeri picked up the coins, closed the book and said, "That was a nice thing to say."

I managed a humble, "Thanks, man."

Although at some level Ray's tribute provided comfort, I felt very much unsettled. I could understand the peace of Ray's path and the creativity of Kirk's, but what about my direction? By leaving the cabin earlier that day I had cut myself off from a dream and set myself adrift. I didn't need the *I Ching* to tell me to leave the cabin, but I hadn't really thought about my next move.

I put my hand out to Jeri. "Here, let me cast them."

Jeri handed me the coins and I threw, yang-yin-yang for the first trigram then yin-yang-yin for the second.

Jeri read from the book. "'Before Completion.' The conditions are difficult. The task is great and full of responsibility. It is nothing less than that of leading the world out of confusion back to order. But it is a task that promises success, because there is a goal that can unite the forces now tending in different directions. At first, however, one must move warily, like an old fox walking over ice. A young fox who as yet has not acquired this caution goes ahead boldly, and it may happen that he falls in and gets his tail wet when he is almost across the water. Then of course his effort has been all in vain. Accordingly, in times 'before completion,' deliberation and caution are the prerequisites of success."

The reading pronounced something I already knew—the path before me held difficulties. Although not consoling, it reinforced my belief in the validity of the divination process. However, the part about "leading the world out of confusion" sounded pretentious, grandiose. I'd withhold judgment on that prediction. I liked the promise of success part, but I feared I might ignore the warning of proceeding carefully and act like the young fox.

# CHAPTER 6

*August 1972, Central PA*

My fiancée, Meryl, finished her music education degree in May and obtained a teaching position in a public school in northcentral Pennsylvania about the same time I left the cabin. Although we were engaged for over two years, we never made any marriage plans because of the uncertainty of our future. Then on a trip to Punxsutawney, PA, where Meryl played organ for a former college roommate's wedding, we got married by a local Justice of the Peace, me in my hiking boots, jeans, and long, dark hair and beard, and Meryl in a hippie "granny gown" and even longer dark hair, with its distinctive gray streak. Her parents wanted a big ceremony, but my status as a drop-out left me not wanting to deal with a social situation where I would be in the spotlight.

The idea of sticking with one girl scares some guys in their twenties, but I had no qualms about marriage. Before we got engaged Meryl and I were together for over three years. I knew that she was the right girl for me even longer, ever since ninth grade. That revelation happened after one Friday night at the spring fling social. I was hanging out with a couple of girls when the DJ announced a "ladies choice."

Meryl, a classmate at that time, and, in fact, all through high school, came over and looked at me with her soft brown eyes and smiled. "Do you want to dance?" she asked.

I'd never flirted with her before, maybe because she got better grades than me. In fact, she got better grades than anyone in our class, a distinction to which I aspired. I swallowed my academic envy and accepted her bidding. As we danced, she sang the wrong words to the record being played. I laughed at her mistake and teased her.

"You don't know that song as well as you think you do."

My short, slightly plump escort shot back, "I wish you were dead."

A bit of an extreme retort for a simple putdown, but hey, we were in ninth grade and academic rivals to boot. I just laughed it off.

The next day I was taken by ambulance to the hospital and diagnosed with meningitis. They announced in school on the following Monday that I was in critical condition and it wasn't certain whether I would make it. I received many get well cards from classmates, but Meryl wrote a letter that touched my heart. Although I didn't realize it then, I fell in love because of that letter.

When I got out of the hospital and returned to school ten days later on the next-to-last day of school, I began flirting with her. We dated off and on for a couple of years before sticking together for good (fifty-three years and counting).

After we eloped, we moved close to the small town of Muncy, just outside of Williamsport, the location of my wife's music teaching job. In the first two years at our new place I had several short-term jobs. I hauled trees on a Christmas tree farm in November and December, then in January I got a job milking cows. Later that year I worked on a construction crew until I was laid off in the fall. I worked on a loading dock at a factory that manufactured furniture in the winter. When spring came around in the second year, construction picked up again and I found another carpentry position. For a guy whose strongest skill had always been his mind, I enjoyed building with my hands and working outside. The new flavors of life tasted good.

# Chapter 7

*July 1974, Central PA*

I didn't make any friends in our two years of living in Muncy, but occasionally reconnected with my old buddy Ray, who had finished his engineering degree. When Ray asked if I would help him move into his new house in Carlisle, PA, that summer, I assured him I would be there.

Since I could walk to my carpentry job, Meryl and I sold our second car to save money. When she needed to attend a class on the Saturday that Ray was moving, I turned to my alternative mode of transportation: hitchhiking. Before I got my car during senior year at Lehigh, I hitchhiked the five-hour trip to Indiana, PA, to visit Meryl on several occasions. Hitching never took me more than twice the time it would take to drive. I wanted to get to Carlisle by 10:00 A.M., the time Ray said they were going to be at the Carlisle location. I figured that leaving by 7:00 A.M. should work for what was normally an hour and a half drive. I hadn't realized the difficulty of hitching in a non-college town environment.

I got up early that Saturday morning in May and stood almost an hour and a half for my first ride, from a guy in a beat up pickup truck, which took me only a third of the way. It took another hour for the second ride, another guy, but this time a nicer truck. This ride only took me to my halfway point, Selinsgrove, a college town. When I had been on the road for over three hours, I finally hitched a ride to my final destination and this time it wasn't a pickup truck, but instead a dirty, brown '67 Plymouth sedan.

The sound of Bachman Turner Overdrive singing "Takin' Care of Business" blasted me as I opened the back, threw my backpack in ahead of me, and hopped onto the seat. "Hey, thanks, guys."

"No problem," the driver shouted before turning down the volume on the radio. "Where you headed?"

"Carlisle."

"Cool, so are we. You going to the car show, too?"

"No, just visiting a friend," I replied.

"Oh, that's cool."

After the car picked up speed the fellow in the passenger seat pulled open a plastic baggie, held it up, and looked at me. "Care to smoke some weed?"

Pot often accompanied hitchhiking in the '70s for dudes with long hair. I didn't skip a beat as I reached in my backpack and pulled out a soapstone pipe, an item I'd carved after Kirk had taught me the basics in stone sculpture. "Here, let's use this. It gives a real smooth smoke," I said as I handed him the pipe.

He took the stone pipe and hefted it in the air twice. The weight appeared to surprise him. "Hey, heavy."

I gave him a puzzled look as if to say, *"Do you mean heavy as in it weighs a lot, or heavy as in the hippie term that means cool and far out at the same time?"*

"Two ways!" he continued as if reading my mind. "Where'd you get it?"

"I carved it myself," I told him, trying not to sound like I was bragging, because cool hippies don't brag. "It's one of the things I'm into." I had the appropriate air of hippie nonchalance.

The obligatory "cool" came back as he filled the pipe and then lit it before taking a toke and passing it around.

We reached Carlisle Fairgrounds and the perpetual traffic snarl that surrounds those events about an hour and a half later. I walked the last mile and a half through the city to Ray's apartment, probably about as fast as driving through the mess would have taken. By the time I reached his place it was 1:00 P.M., five hours after I left for what should have been an hour and a half trip for anyone driving straight through.

Any thought that a bit of cannabis might perk me up turned out to be a serious error. By the time I reached Ray's I was dehydrated and hungry, with a really bad headache and my carpenter's shoulder throbbing. I knocked on the door at the address that Ray had given me and prayed that a friendly face would appear. I hoped they wouldn't be out picking up another load to move from the old place to the new.

After several more knocks and about three minutes of waiting, I gave one final loud knock, and then with a reluctant sigh turned around and looked down the street to plan where I might go to find something to eat, when Kris finally came to the door.

"Oh, you *are* here!" I exclaimed. "I've been knocking and knocking."

"Yes, we've been back in the kitchen. We just heard your knock," she told me. "Come on in. You look terrible," she said as we embraced. "Can I get you something to eat?"

"That would be fantastic!" I told her. "I'm starving. And do you have some water? I'm dying for a drink."

"Sure, come on." She motioned me to the kitchen where Ray sat at the table.

"Hey, Beaky," Ray greeted me with my college nickname bestowed after a group of us watched the 1941 Hitchcock flick *Suspicion*. "Good to see you, man. It's been too long."

Kris handed me a glass of water.

"Thanks," I told her and took a long swallow. "Ah!" I let out a satisfied sigh as I put the glass down on the table.

"Sit down," Kris told me. "We have some Chinese take-out left over from our lunch. Do you want some?"

"Sure. Thanks. That'd be great," I assured her as I sat down.

She got the food out of the refrigerator, picked up a plastic fork, put it in the food container, and handed it to me.

I ate and regained some energy as they related their moving adventure. Turned out that Ray's brother and brother-in-law had come through with a truck and crew of guys and the moving had all been done by noon. We had the afternoon to just sit around and talk and enjoy each other's company before my wife arrived to pick me up after her class.

At the end of the day, it became quite apparent that Ray, who was now a civil engineer at a large prestigious engineering firm, had grown in a direction that diverged about as far as possible from my wandering existence. He was on the fast track to a successful career, while I, the dropout, couldn't keep a steady job. Our lives had taken such different paths that I knew the closeness we had once felt would likely never rematerialize. That realization saddened me and made me feel isolated, but rather than wallow in self-pity, I attempted to glory in that solitude.

# Chapter 8

*October 1977, Rural Lycoming County, PA*

*Hoo, Hoo, Hoooooooot.*
*Hoo, Hoot.*

I looked in the direction of the sound. The moonlight provided just enough glow to make out the silhouette of a great horned owl, perched on a lone tree branch. I didn't divert my path, but kept trudging at a jog along the edge of the field next to a row of tall trees. When I reached the pile of rocks that marked the edge of the field and the beginning of the woods, I peered back for another glance at the source of the haunting call.

*Hoo, hooooo, hoo.*

The bird seemed to bid farewell. I kept my focus on the terrain ahead, now more than before, as the shadows from the tree branches blotted out all but a few rays of moonlight. I knew these woods well enough to be bushwhacking, following no trail. In another two hundred or so yards I would reach the creek. I kept jogging with high steps. The area wasn't rocky, but plenty of fallen trees made the passage tricky. It would have been a challenge in full daylight. The lack of daylight made it dangerous, but that was the idea.

I felt like I needed to take risks if I wanted to follow Castaneda's "Path with Heart." For the last three years, whenever I could, I roamed the woods in northcentral Pennsylvania looking for guidance in the words of Carlos Castaneda and the lessons from his teacher, Don Juan, a Yaqui Indian sorcerer, or shaman. Now I was doing what Castaneda called "The Gait of Power," running in the woods in the darkness.

When I came to the creek, I continued without hesitation. The chilly stream provided a contrast to the warm October evening. I took a short, quick breath when the shocking temperature hit me. As the stream level rose over my knees, the resistance of the water slowed me down. When it came up to mid-thigh the current became so strong that I had to fight to maintain my balance.

In less than five seconds my jog turned into a crawl. I struggled for each step, leaning into the flow and pawing the bottom with my feet, trying to feel where I could secure footing for the next step. I felt a surge of adrenaline as I battled the swift flow of water. After several very long seconds, I passed through the deepest area and wallowed to the stream's edge. I grabbed a tree root and vaulted onto the four-foot-high bank.

I resumed my jog through the dense woods, water now squishing from my boots. As I neared the edge of the field that led to my home, I knew I only had about one hundred yards of forest to negotiate before the end of my three-mile jaunt. I picked up the pace. Not a good idea.

*Whack!* I hit my shin against a fallen tree.

"Aaaah! Shhhhhi..."

I suppressed a curse and kept on going without looking at my injury. My leg throbbed, but I wanted to ignore the pain. Castaneda's teacher had insisted that "stopping the inner dialogue" was a key step in becoming a "warrior." I fought the urge to chastise my stupidity for being so reckless and kept going, but at a slower pace. When I reached the field I could see the porch light at our place. I stopped jogging and walked the last short distance home with a slight limp.

Castaneda's bizarre view of existence enchanted me. I walked the back roads, fields, and woods of rural northern Pennsylvania under his inspiration and influence, spending hours trying to stop my internal dialogue, looking for the "warrior's path."

Castaneda spoke of how shamans could directly perceive the lines of energy that flowed throughout the universe, and how they also could see humans as luminous balls of energy. At times it felt as though I made fleeting progress in this. Occasionally I saw people as luminous balls with lines emanating from the midsection as Castaneda had described. This had nothing to do with drugs, and seemed to only happen when I succeeded in stopping my inner discourse. But I couldn't control these occurrences, and I wasn't convinced I was seeing something real. Maybe it was a hallucination appearing only because of Castaneda's suggestion.

In any event, that night I felt dejected. My efforts to become a warrior seemed in vain. All I had to show was a sore leg. I opened the door and entered. I could tell my wife had not yet arrived, since the car was not in the driveway. I changed into dry clothes and went into the room where I had been painting before I left for my power gait.

"I'm back," my wife announced several minutes later, as she entered the front door of the house trailer we rented and currently called home.

I gave the painting I'd been working on a puzzled look, as if to say *"What the heck is it?"* before putting my paint brush in the container of water. Then I wiped my hands on my spill rag and hurried out to the living room where I greeted my love with a big hug.

"Did you get enlightened?" I asked, poking fun at her latest adventure, a trip to Philadelphia to attend a conference sponsored by the Yoga Research Society. She'd learned about the conference from her yoga instructor, who was a member. Her instructor's teacher, or rather guru, was the head of the society, which was centered in Philly.

"It was fantastic," she said. "I want to tell you all about it." Then she held out a bag. "Here are some books I bought there. I think you might like them."

I raised an eyebrow and cocked my head to one side. I didn't share her enthusiasm for her yoga practice. The only book I'd read on yoga seemed shallow, focused solely on postures with no philosophy like what I found intriguing with the Ram Dass story. I assumed her yoga classes would not lead to anything that could hold my interest.

"They just seemed to be calling your name, so I had to get them," she said with a smile and pushed the bag of books closer to me.

I warmed up to her earnestness and returned her smile. "Oh, really?" I took the bag from her and removed the books.

"I really felt that you should have these," she said, pointing to *The Fourth Way* and *In Search of the Miraculous*, books written by P.D. Ouspensky, a student of the Russian philosopher G.I. Gurdjieff.

In the five years since Ram Dass's story about raja yoga inspired me to drop out of school, my quest for spiritual growth had narrowed. I'd given up on meditation and the *I Ching*. Only Castaneda's work still inspired me. It motivated me to wander for miles and miles each day throughout the countryside trying to adopt the persona of a "warrior," as if searching for the ghost of Don Juan.

Meryl had supported and stood by me through our five years of marriage, even though I never held any job longer than three months. Now she proved to be doing more than just standing by me. She brought something I truly needed. She carried home from Philadelphia a fresh set of ideas that held a new way for me to interpret my world.

New knowledge and understanding concerning body and spirit can come from a flesh and blood teacher with direct experience on the matter, or through an impersonal book. There are pros and cons about information gained through a book. When reading material intended to teach about spiritual practices, you can't tell whenever you interpret a lesson incorrectly. Without feedback from someone who knows the material, you might believe that you have mastered a complex concept or practice, when instead you have traveled down a long and twisted road leading in the wrong direction. With hindsight I see that this often happened to me with these books, but that didn't deter me from wandering with abandon into their depths.

Having a manuscript as a teacher does have an upside. You don't have to worry about a personal relationship with another human being. None of that *"Am I pleasing my guru or not?"* anguish. This relationship absence left open the opportunity for me to use these books to develop a deeper, more spiritual relationship with my wife. This proved as important to my emotional growth and well-being as the information found in the books was for my intellectual development.

The next day I started reading the first of the new books, *Yoga and Psychotherapy*, written by Swami Rama the leader of the Himalayan Institute. I had a void to fill. I held no job, couldn't tolerate TV, and had given up on reading. In the summer I spent most non-roaming time in our large vegetable garden, but since the fall, I resorted to painting to fill time, a fruitless effort for someone with my limited abilities in that arena.

"I didn't realize that in yoga psychology you have something close to the id, ego, and superego," I told Meryl.

"How's that?" my wife asked as she sat on the couch crocheting an afghan.

"They're talking about people having several bodies. There's the physical body, the energy body, and the mental body," I told her. "The physical body is like the id, with all the instinctual stuff going on. You know... gotta eat, gotta have sex, gotta survive. The mental body fits, sort of, with the superego. I mean, the superego is supposed to be the part of you that thinks about how you should behave, so it seems to do most of the mental work. The ego on the other hand just acts impulsively to self-gratify or self-aggrandize, so it seems to co-opt all of the energy. Oh, another name they give for the energy body is the astral body."

"But don't they think of these bodies as separate? Aren't you supposed to be able to travel in the astral body? Freud's id, ego, and superego are thought of as just parts of a whole, right?" She used the intonation of a question, but in reality was pointing out a fact that contradicted my observation.

"Yeah, you're right."

I hated ever to admit that she was right when she corrected me. That desire of each of us to top the other went back to high school, but at least it wasn't a testosterone battle like with another guy. With my wife the mental battles just seemed to be sparks that kindled a deeper fire.

As usual I didn't let my concession be the last word. "But it's interesting that there are three distinct entities and the functions match up."

After thinking for a few seconds I continued the thread. "There are two other significant differences between Freud and the yoga psychology of this book, besides what you pointed out."

"Oh, what are they?" she asked, as she first pulled more thick, orange yarn from the skein and then with her crochet hook formed another knot, and another.

"One is the relationships between the three parts. For Freud the superego has to mediate between the ego and the id, but the book says the energy body mediates between the physical and the mental."

When she didn't look up from her work, I continued. "The other thing is that Freud, and Western psychology in general, focuses on the limitations and illness of the mind, while yoga psychology focuses on the possibility of raising your consciousness and evolving beyond normal awareness in this world, escaping the confines of the ego."

"Which makes it more personal," she said.

"What do you mean?"

She waited until she reached the end of a row before looking up from her work and answering. "Well, if psychology is just about how wacko or weird people are, I would think you would be less likely to be thinking about how to relate to it. But if you are reading about how a person can evolve, that can grab you and pull you in."

I nodded, but didn't really understand the truth of her statement. The book had already exerted great influence on me. "It says that you can learn to control your astral body with prana, which is just breath control. If you learn the right exercises, you can separate the astral body from the physical."

A second theme of *Yoga and Psychotherapy* concerned chakras. "You know anything about chakras?" I asked my wife later that month.

"I've heard the term used in yoga class," she replied, looking up from the book she was reading. "Why? What's it say about them?"

"According to the book, the body has seven chakras that correspond with major nerve centers. The first chakra is located by the anus and has connections with fear and aggression." I paused. "That makes sense." I said after a bit of reflection. "You know the saying 'keep a tight asshole'?"

"No, can't say as I do," she said, not sounding amused.

"It was in Norman Mailer's book *The Naked and the Dead*. Supposed to be something soldiers told each other before battle. Like don't shit your pants out of fear. I remember one time running in Muncy and a dog charged out after me. I had to tighten up my sphincter to keep my pants clean."

I got a raised eyebrow from my wife. When she didn't offer any comments I continued. "The genitals are the second chakra. Goes from fear to ecstasy," I murmured. "Okay. Here's one that's interesting. The area around the navel corresponds to the third chakra. It's supposed to be the seat of the will. What's interesting is that this chakra is supposed to connect to other centers via lines of energy. This fits with Castaneda's description of lines of force emanating from the naval. Don Juan said that a sorcerer could see these lines."

I got an uninterested, "Oh," from my wife.

Meryl didn't share my affinity for Castaneda. She saw my fascination with his books as something that distanced us. I didn't relate the fleeting glimpses of such lines that I had experienced, but just thought to myself that maybe what I'd seen was based on something other than fantasy.

According to Swami Rama and his co-authors, the first three chakras have connections to the instincts. The diaphragm, the muscle responsible for breathing, separates the lower three chakras from the higher chakras, where higher consciousness takes place. Through proper breathing techniques one can learn to elevate energy, or prana, from the lower chakras to the higher ones. If enough energy does not reach the fourth chakra a person appears emotionless and cold.

The fourth chakra, the heart chakra, controls love and sensitivity of feelings for others. Nurturance and creativity occur in the fifth, the throat chakra, located in the area of the thyroid gland. The sixth charka, also known as the third eye, resides by the pineal gland. In this chakra intuitive knowledge develops and the experience of higher consciousness takes place. At the final chakra, located at the crown of the skull, the differentiation between the experiencer and experienced ceases to exist.

The authors of *Yoga and Psychotherapy* called the chakras a "playroom… a workshop or laboratory within which [a person] can experiment with experiencing and expressing different aspects of his being." Naïve to the inherent dangers in running such experiments unsupervised, I pursued this avenue with abandon, working with breathing and mental exercises in an effort to move prana into the higher chakras. I attempted some powerful breathing techniques, a bit like playing with fire, since I didn't have a teacher to explain them properly. But I also didn't have inhibitions to keep me from exploring. My awareness of chakras and energy movement grew, however, not in a way that I could say I fully understood.

Through certain breathing exercises that focused my attention on chakras, I grew an awareness of a source of energy that seemed to emanate from my navel area. Years later a biologist, Michael Gershon, identified in his 1996 book *The Second Brain* a "second brain" in humans. The enteric nervous system consists of 100 million neurons located in the gut and it controls bodily functions related to digestion. Somehow this brain took over the role of my rational brain in my head when it came to issues of eating. My gut brain wouldn't let my thinking brain eat just anything. I would get signals for and against food options. I ate less and less, and then only raw fruits and vegetables and sprouted grains. My weight, which had been a lean 155 pounds as a five-foot ten-inch athlete in high school, had dropped to 145 as I walked hours on end in recent years. Now as I worked on my chakras it fell to 135 pounds.

With the loss of weight came a gain in awareness. My sensitivities to sensory input heightened. I could hear sounds that my wife never registered. When the refrigerator motor cycled on, I would take notice even from three rooms away. My perceptiveness of other persons' emotional and mental states also increased. My radar could pick up signs from my wife when something was troubling her before the issue reached a point where we needed to talk about it.

But any idea that I was becoming an advanced master was usually put to rest in short order by some foolish or inattentive act on my part.

# CHAPTER 9

*November 1977, Rural Lycoming County, PA*

The fourteen by seventy-foot mobile home where we lived sat on the corner of a lot beside an old farmhouse. Only two years earlier the landlord put it there, straight from the factory, for his aging parents. It became vacant when the elderly couple divorced, after over fifty years of marriage. Not an auspicious act to follow, but we moved into our fourth home in five years before finding out its history. Not that it would have stopped us from living there. We liked the country location with only one neighbor—our landlord, a farmer, who lived a short distance away.

We felt comfortable in our problem-free new home initially, but a few weeks after my wife's Philadelphia trip, our kitchen sink backed up. The problem stemmed from inadequate pitch in the drainage line. We told the landlord about the issue, and then adapted to the practice of emptying the sink by carrying pots full of dirty water to the toilet down the hall, where the drainage was not affected.

Two days of lack of kitchen sink drainage passed and my wife left for work as usual. I had no idea that the landlord had decided to fix the drainage problem that particular day. My daily practices at that time included yoga exercises. In a single-wide mobile home the options for stretching out to do yoga are limited to one space, the living room, and even there the coffee table needed to be pushed back against the couch before I could do yoga poses like the cobra or locust.

I always practiced my yoga postures by myself, and because I wanted to feel as comfortable as possible, over time my manner of dress had evolved from sweat suit to shorts to nothing. I found clothing interfered with my awareness of the position of my body and how to best control its movements.

As I lay naked in the middle of the living room floor, I heard the landlord and his son talking in the driveway outside the trailer. At first I ignored them and kept my focus on my yoga posture and the breathing exercise I developed for raising the prana. Then I heard footsteps coming up my front porch and a loud knock on the door. Instead of yelling *"Just a minute"* and scrambling to get dressed, I stayed frozen in my pose. I thought that staying low to the floor was the best course of action—or should I say inaction. The front windows could be viewed from the front porch, and I thought that if I got up to grab my clothes from the couch I would be seen. Little did I think that the landlord's son would just burst into the trailer... but without any warning he did. Of course, once he saw me lying naked on the floor he immediately left. With that I snatched my clothing and got dressed, a little late.

Embarrassing moments notwithstanding, I continued my esoteric studies unfazed. After finishing the Swami Rama volume I moved on to Patanjali's *Yogi Sutras*, translated and with commentary by Taimni, titled *The Science of Yoga*. Each of Patanjali's 195 sutras contained a single, simple sentence. The sutras together form the discipline of raja yoga, a classic path over 2,000 years old. I first heard of this path in the Ram Dass tapes, and then in the book *Yoga and Psychotherapy*, which devoted many pages to Patanjali and his work. The sutras, along with a generous dose of commentary by Taimni, gave substance to the ideas I had found captivating in Ram Dass, Castaneda, and *Yoga and Psychotherapy*. They provided more fuel for the fire of self-seeking already lit within me.

Patanjali defined yoga as the cessation of the modifications of the mind. Essentially the same goal that Ram Dass and Castaneda pursued, but from Ram Dass all that I learned was "be here now" while Castaneda admonished me to "stop the inner dialogue." Both clearly stated goals but no instructions. With Patanjali I got more than a goal; I got a blueprint for attaining it. The sutras identified the types of modifications of the mind and practical methods for how they can be controlled. The book gave a list of practical observances to undertake and also expounded on a system of metaphysics that explained consciousness and the purpose of life far better to me than the Judeo-Christian way I had learned growing up. Swami Rama provided a bridge from Western psychology to yoga, and *The Science of Yoga* picked me up at the end of that bridge and carried me deep into the forest of yoga thought. So deep I could not have found my way out on my own, had I wanted, but I didn't feel lost, only enchanted.

My work on chakras and my esoteric books took up an increasing amount of my time and affected my lifestyle choices. I had long since quit drinking any alcohol, not that I ever partook of it much anyway. Now I gave up caffeine. Not too difficult for someone who gets jumpy on just half a cup of coffee. I threw away the pipe I hand-carved from soapstone and my stash of pot. This took more conviction, since Ram Dass talked of doing psychedelic drugs while seriously studying yoga, and Castaneda's initiation into sorcery involved ceremonial peyote.

In the past I grew my own ceremonial cannabis down along the Susquehanna River and smoked it on rare occasions. But finally I came to the conclusion: no more marijuana for me. The last smoke I indulged in was the only one I took after beginning to read the books my wife brought home from Philly. That time my THC high let me think I discovered a magical truth, but soon after the peak of the experience I realized the only thing I had revealed to myself was that pot makes you believe in nonsensical things.

Not only did I modify what I chose to put into my body, but I altered my surroundings, too. I threw away a hundred-year-old cast iron bank that my grandmother had given me. Once an antique dealer had offered me $125 for the bank, which consisted of a figure on a mule where you put a coin in the figure's mouth. If you pressed a button on its base, the mule kicked its back legs up, dismounted the rider, and as a result the coin fell through the slot and into the bank's repository. The figure was a caricature of a diminutive black man. Throwing away this artifact of racism made me feel liberated from a cultural burden.

My weight plummeted to 125 pounds.

# Chapter 10

*December 1977, Rural Lycoming County, PA*

Living in rural northcentral Pennsylvania does not afford one with many opportunities for cultural events. Yes, there is bingo at the fire hall every Friday night, and on the fourth Saturday you can take in a square dance at the local grange, but nothing too fancy for the pickup truck folks with their gun racks and flag decals. Occasionally, though, one of the small colleges in the area presented a program that provided a more flavorful offering aimed at the liberal-minded minority.

As a music teacher, my wife had eclectic tastes. She could certainly enjoy the hoedown music at the square dance, but she also appreciated classical and avant garde music and arts. So when Susquehanna University booked the Alvin Ailey dance troop that fall, we jumped at the chance to go. We even called a longtime friend who lived about an hour away and asked her to join us.

"So you two are still together?" Elise asked in a rhetorical manner after greeting us. She'd eloped at about the same time that we had, but her marriage ended in divorce over a year earlier.

"Guess so," I replied with a grin.

"Yep," my wife agreed with equanimity. She still stood with me, even though I hadn't worked a paying job for over two years. Our relationship even improved with her introduction of the esoteric studies. She could see the effort I put into a spiritual quest that we both shared. Although I wasn't contributing financially, at least I wasn't out drinking and womanizing.

"So any thoughts on having children?" Elise asked, the perennial question for childless couples who have been married for five years.

"No," my wife told her, sounding disappointed as she opened the closet to get out her coat. Although she hadn't said anything about becoming parents recently, I knew she wanted to become a mother.

"Not going to happen," I said.

"You never know," Elise said, giving my wife a wink. "There can always be an accident."

I raised my eyebrows. "In order for there to be an accident there has to be a certain biological connection between the man and woman." I got my coat and we all walked out the door.

"Yes, but I've always found that the man is more than willing to make that biological connection," she said with a smile as she headed to where the cars were parked.

"We'll take ours," I told her, motioning toward our vehicle. The brisk air of late fall felt refreshing as we got in the '70 Opel and started off. "Well, I haven't made the biological connection for three months," I told her, getting back to our conversation as we turned out of our lane onto the dirt road that ran by our trailer.

"Really, celibacy?" she said with an incredulous look. "Why?"

"He's into the yamas of yoga," my wife told her.

"Oh, yoga," Elise said with a knowing nod. "Yes, I should have known from looking at those eyes of yours. They reminded me of the people who surrounded Maharaji." After a few seconds she addressed my wife. "The yamas of yoga?"

I intercepted the question. "You didn't get into the yamas and niyamas when you were a follower of Maharaji?" I asked.

"No. We just got our individualized mantra, plenty of talks about being in the moment, and other useful philosophical advice, but nothing called yamas or niyamas."

We had reached the end of the dirt road, and after stopping I pulled out onto the blacktop that led toward the main highway. "Well, the yamas and niyamas are the first two of the eight limbs of Patanjali's yoga. They are like the ten commandments of yoga. Some of them are the same as Moses's ten. The yamas are the 'thou shalt nots' of yoga. Thou shall not do violence, lie, steal, be possessive, or do sensual stuff. Thus, no sex. The niyamas are listed as observances. These include purity, contentment, austerity, self-study, and surrender to God." I paused and laughed. "So, no having fun and indulging yourself, basically," I concluded.

I'd gotten the extreme interpretation of celibacy as the second yama, brahmacharya, from the *The Science of Yoga*. Perhaps a more moderate reading of abstinence from excessive sex, or lustfulness, would have served me better, but at least for nine months of my life this viewpoint held sway.

"So you better not have fun tonight, then," she said in mock seriousness.

"Wouldn't think of it," I rejoined. "It's all self-study tonight."

# Chapter 11

*February 1978, Rural Lycoming County, PA*

After finishing *The Science of Yoga*, two books remained, both by P. D. Ouspensky. My wife thought I should really have these, but each time I picked up one of them it felt as though some force took hold of me. I found it physically difficult to open these texts, as though my arms had lead weights attached. Thus, I had opted for reading the others first. I tried to analyze why this happened. Was I just being contrary? My wife and I often resisted something the other suggested, due to our stubborn nature and our history of competition, but we had shared so much with the first two books that I couldn't accept that explanation. With an uneasy feeling I forced myself to push through the physical repulsion and open the first book.

*In Search of the Miraculous* depicts P. D. Ouspensky's time with someone he called "G," starting when the two met in St. Petersburg, Russia, just before the revolution in 1917. When the text came to the part where the two made a harrowing escape from the Bolsheviks through the Caucasus Mountains, I had to put the book down. The story numbed me to a point where I found it difficult to continue.

Why couldn't I bring myself to read this? I couldn't answer this question. I only knew that reading the passage evoked a distant memory I couldn't quite place into context, as though I'd read about a difficult personal experience that I didn't want to recall.

Unwilling to deal with the stress it produced, I put *The Search* aside and took up *The Fourth Way*, a book on the teachings of G. I. Gurdjieff. The passages gripped me. The lessons seemed to dovetail with all the previous ones on yoga. It gave practical ways to confront the trials of living in the world, but I could only read a small section at one sitting. If I tried to race on to read more, my eyes would freeze, and I would go into a trancelike state. If I willed myself to move my eyes and read further, I would immediately get an acute headache, painful enough that I had to stop.

A practice of slow reading developed into a routine. I would read a passage and become numb, unable to do anything. This stupor, which left me feeling intoxicated, would last quite some time before I could begin reading again. At the time this process happened I had no comprehension of what was taking place. Why couldn't I read this book and digest it with the same speed that I had done with the two books on yoga? I could only attribute this mandatory snail-paced reading to the density of the content. By reading at a slow pace I absorbed these new, deep ideas better. Was my subconscious forcing me to keep this pace for some other reason?

Gurdjieff emphasized self-study, and insisted that one cannot "do" anything without it. I followed this advice while reading; not because I chose to, but because something forced me. I felt as if under a spell when reading his teachings. Nothing I had ever read before affected me in such a way.

Gurdjieff claimed that in order to "do" anything a person first had to know how to control negative emotions. Without such control a person merely reacted to his or her environment, not really exercising control. This made clear sense to me. At this point in my life I did not feel that I had control of my destiny, and that feeling spawned many negative thoughts and emotions. Lack of personal control and negative feelings seemed inexorably intertwined. If I could expel negativity from my thoughts and feelings, I believed that I could get my life in a position where I did have control.

## June 1978

My weight dropped to 113 pounds. What I interpreted as progress in personal development and understanding of chakras and prana, others most likely saw as anorexia. But others rarely did see me. Without a job I had no need to leave the trailer and we had few visitors. Those who did come usually saw me in a loose fitting, long, brown robe that Meryl had sewn for me. It helped hide the fact that I was forty-five pounds below my ideal weight. Along with my long hair and beard I looked like one of those gaunt yogis Westerners have seen in photos that people in India encounter on a regular basis.

I withdrew into my own world of chakras and prana, tracking the energy flowing throughout my body more and more. My connection to the "real world" was my wife. Our relationship stayed strong. I had given up job seeking and now just helped around the house, even making my wife's lunch to carry to school. We both had taken to eating only raw foods. Our fridge always held a wide variety of raw fruits and veggies, and my wife appreciated my efforts to have something ready for her before she left for work.

Most of my time during the day was spent seeking enlightenment through meditation and breathing practices. I suppose I wanted an intuitive flash, some dramatic revelation that would signify an astonishing change in me. For certain I didn't want to dwell on the fact that I felt my status in the world was a nothing. I fought that negative image on a regular basis.

Gurdjieff claimed that before you could gain control of negative emotions you had to understand what caused them. Once a negative emotion had taken hold of you, you could do nothing but endure it. To control negative feelings you had to learn what triggered them, and then you might be able to prevent the trigger from being pulled. At first, though, you could only watch yourself. I paid close attention to the source of my negative feelings in the context of energy transfer between chakras.

Somehow this effort to exile negativity led me to cut my shoulder-length hair, not in a fully conscious manner, but rather, one afternoon the energy led me to a pair of scissors. In short order I saw a stranger staring back at me from the mirror. I lost my identity as a hippie seeker. With nothing anchoring me to this world it felt as though I would float or sail away. My wife's assurances that evening that I looked "great" did not take away my emptiness. I felt adrift.

# Chapter 12

*June 1978, Rural Lycoming County, PA*

The day after I cut my hair I called my wife where she taught.

"Honey, hey, uh... could you come home right now? I am not feeling too good." I paused for a second, listening to the silence on the other end.

My wife had been pulled from her first afternoon classroom by a message that she had an urgent call from home. She did not make an immediate response to my request.

"My head feels funny," I continued, trying to sound apologetic.

"But I'm at work," she finally blurted out. "Do you want me to call an ambulance?"

"No. I just want you to come here to me," I said softly.

"Why?" she asked, her incredulity clearly showing.

I raised my voice, a bit frustrated. "I told you. My head doesn't feel right."

"Why don't you take something for it? That's what medicine is for," she said, but she knew that I probably would not take any pills on principle, since I never did. "I can't come home now. I have to teach."

I paused before responding, considering what to say. "Well, can't you take personal leave?" I asked. "It's the end of the year." My wife kept silent again still trying to make sense of the phone call. "It's not like they'll miss you," I told her.

"Can't you just wait a couple more hours until I get off?" she asked, her incredulity turning to annoyance.

I pleaded this time. "No. I need you now."

I clearly sounded distressed, but she could not comprehend why I wanted her. "Are you sure? I don't want to have to ask anyone for personal leave," she tried again. "Can't you just wait?"

"No. Please come now." My voice pleaded, sounding weak. "I feel like I have never felt before. It's kind of scary and I want you here. Please." My insistence wore on my wife. She finally capitulated.

"Well, okay," she said. "I'll be there if I can get them to let me take leave."

When she got home about twenty-five minutes later, I greeted her by the driveway where I had been sitting for some time in the warm and sunny, early June afternoon awaiting her arrival.

"I felt really strange leaving work," she said through the open window as she pulled the car to a stop at the end of the driveway.

"I'm sorry," I said. I looked down at my feet, unable to meet her gaze. "My head feels like the top of it is about to push out." I picked up a dandelion from the lawn in front of me that had gone to seed and picked a few white tufted seed pods, tossing them in the air.

She looked at me in disbelief. "Why? What do you mean? Did you do something to your head?" She got out of the car, closed the door, and walked to where I was sitting.

I stammered as I picked more of the white tops of dandelion seeds. "I don't know. Why? Ah, er... no." I blew on the seeds and they floated away in the gentle breeze. "I mean, no, I didn't do anything. I don't know what's wrong. It just feels like I am about to join the ocean of consciousness. Go over to the other side."

Her disbelief deepened as she stopped in front of me. "What ocean? The other side of what? You aren't making sense." She studied me for a moment. "What did you eat today?" She knew I had strange eating habits and wondered if that could account for my puzzling behavior.

I couldn't make a connection to her question about what I ate or how I was feeling, so I connected it to what I was doing. "*Dandy lion* seeds," I said, and raised my eyebrows as I took a few dandelion seeds off of the flower and put them into my mouth.

"Don't do that," she snapped, her patience wearing thin. "Quit acting weird."

"Why? They're good," I mocked seriousness as I plucked another pinch of the seeds into my mouth. I ignored the unpleasantness of their dry, wispy, dust-like texture and pretended to savor them. "*Mmm.*" My attempt at humor failed to ease the tension between us.

"What's your problem?" She confronted me, stepping up close. "Why did you call me home?"

"I told you. I feel really strange. It feels like my spine is splitting open into two parts... like nothing I can explain." This time I looked at her and smiled.

"Do you want me to take you to a doctor?" She appeared a bit calmer, disarmed by my smile, I suppose.

"No, I don't want to see any doctor. They wouldn't understand what I am going through." I believed my experience had something to do with consciousness expansion that Western medicine did not subscribe to.

"Well, then, what do you want me to do?"

I didn't hesitate. "Take me to SKY Land," I replied.

"No. I don't want to take you there. It's not a health center," she said. "It's a retreat where people go to practice yoga, and besides, there isn't any program going on there now. Greg is probably busy getting ready for the summer program."

"But he will understand me," I responded. Greg taught yoga and ran SKY Land. He possessed advanced knowledge in esoteric matters. I'd visited him the previous winter and he had given me a personal yoga lesson. "And maybe I can help him get ready for the summer. I could volunteer. I'm sure he could use some help, and maybe all I need is something to do."

Meryl studied me for several long seconds before responding. "Well, okay. Let me get ready. I want to eat first, or at least take something to eat. If we leave now it will be just about suppertime when we get there," she said as she started toward the front door. "You better change into something more presentable," she mentioned causally. "Those shorts look a bit nerdy." With the warmer weather I had traded my long robe for a pair of loose-fitting shorts.

"Oh, these will be fine. There isn't going to be anyone except Greg and Julie," I said as I followed her.

She looked at me and rolled her eyes before entering the house, as if to say, *"No use arguing with you in that state."*

# CHAPTER 13

*June 1978, Rural Columbia County, PA*

The drive to Greg's took a little over an hour. SKY Land, a 250-acre farm in northern Columbia County, held summer retreats sponsored by the Swami Kyuvyanada Yoga foundation—SKY for short. The compound of buildings—two homes, a barn, a garage, and a half dozen other smaller buildings—sat in the middle of a small valley. From these buildings the farm stretched out in all directions as far as one could see, with no neighboring land visible at all. Hills rose on both sides of the dirt road which entered woods in both directions. Two spring-fed ponds located close to the buildings capped the idyllic scene.

Greg had ambitious plans. For himself he wanted to achieve enlightenment, as conceived by yoga practitioners. For his farm he wanted to turn it into a retreat that would attract students and provide them with an ideal setting to learn and practice yoga. He already had renovated several outbuildings for various uses. He recently finished the Asana Hall, the main venue for yoga classes. Another building served as a library and small dorm. Several other dorm projects awaited, along with organic garden development and other general improvements.

We arrived after suppertime after stopping to eat some dried fruit and nuts along the way, not an unusual meal for us at the time as we ate an almost all raw vegetarian diet. Greg had not yet returned from the evening yoga class that he taught at a nearby college, so we talked with Julie until his arrival. His class lasted until 9 P.M. and he had a half-hour drive, making it rather late to come home to visitors.

"What are you doing here?" Greg's terse voice boomed upon entering the front door and seeing uninvited guests in his living room. He stretched tall his six-foot frame and pulled back his shoulders to reveal an imposing, well-sculpted physique beneath a tight-fitting t-shirt. Then he gave a nervous look to his wife who was seven months pregnant. "Are you okay?"

Julie, noting his protective stance, interjected, "It's okay. I'm fine."

"I wanted to see you and maybe get some more advice." I hoped the embarrassment in my voice would calm him down.

"Why didn't you call and make an appointment?" he barked, still annoyed.

"It's okay, Greg," Julie again came to my defense. "He has an urgent need to find answers." In the hours before Greg's arrival we had discussed the feelings that had brought me there.

Greg gave his wife a puzzled look, and then turned to me and spoke in a somewhat gentler but still authoritative voice. "What's the issue?" Then before I could answer he gestured toward the kitchen and said, "Come on, let's go out to the kitchen. I haven't had anything to eat since lunch."

He got some yogurt from the refrigerator, while I opened a bag of our dried fruit and offered it to him. "These are delicious. All organic," I told him.

He took a handful and said, "Thanks." Then he sat down at the kitchen table and continued, "Now, tell me why you're here."

I explained how I felt, the head exploding, the spine splitting, going over to the ocean. He listened intently as he ate, and when I finished he exclaimed, "Wow, you don't know how powerful that makes me feel that you chose to come here when you felt that way!"

The statement took me aback. I had expected a response with a bit more understanding or compassion, instead of a self-aggrandizing retort. Before I could dwell on the surprising response, it got even weirder.

"You know what you described reminds me of a fellow in India that I read about," he continued. "This guy had experiences similar to what you just told me, about joining the ocean of consciousness, and he traveled all over India just talking to people and explaining how he had been transformed." Greg started into the details of this traveler, about how he dressed, and the way people reacted and how it changed him. He talked uninterrupted for several minutes relaying the story.

I struggled with disbelief, uncertain how to catalogue the tale. Was he trying to discourage my behavior? Was he trying to encourage it? I couldn't make sense of his story.

"Maybe you'll start going around like this, too," he said with apparent sincerity as he finished his monologue and took another bite of food.

I couldn't tell if he was serious. It didn't seem possible, but his tone didn't betray humor. I just gave him a blank look. Such a thought couldn't have been further from my mind.

After some hesitation I said, "I don't think so. Not soon, anyhow, I hope."

Greg managed a smile. "You don't think?" he chuckled, letting me in on the joke.

"I was thinking that maybe I just needed some physical work to do. That maybe I was just getting too much into my head," I said, looking down.

Greg continued to eat, while looking at me with what I sensed as skepticism. When my subtleness failed to elicit a response, I pressed my point. "I wonder if you might need somebody to help around the farm to get ready for the summer program. I have some experience doing carpentry work."

Greg chewed another bite of his food and looked thoughtful. When he finished chewing he spoke in a matter-of-fact manner. "Well, I have most things ready for the summer. I could have used you two weeks ago when I installed the dry wall in the Asana Hall." He paused a bit before adding, "I suppose there are a few things that you could help out on." He looked unconvinced about the wisdom of letting someone work for him, but unwilling to simply dismiss the idea. "What have you been doing lately?" he asked.

I explained my recent mental activity and esoteric involvement with Swami Rama and the Patanjali sutras. This touched a hot button of his and he again went into a long discourse on the yoga sutras and their significance in relation to my experiences. I listened as he interpreted different sutras and noted how incorrect interpretations and practices stemming from such mistaken ideas could land a person in trouble.

I couldn't really appreciate the warnings because of my agitated state of mind, although looking back, this insight made evident sense. However, his words at the time only created a feeling of disdain for his lecturing style. It seemed to me that his tongue wagged on and on. Finally, as he concluded his counsel, which I perceived as a mini-sermon, he asked, "Do you follow me?"

I sat in stone-faced silence for a few seconds for dramatic effect before answering without any expression, "Don't lead. Don't follow." I wanted to be treated like an equal, not as a fool who had stumbled into his midst, as in reality I had done. I felt defensive about my understanding of the yoga sutras and my esoteric practices with chakras. I imagined that I knew these matters rather well, having studied them intensely over the past several months, and I didn't want anyone talking to me like I didn't.

Greg looked miffed at my twisting of his question. "No," he corrected my interpretation of his question. "Do you understand what I'm saying?"

"Yes, I understand you," I told him, still not smiling.

Greg must have interpreted the dissonance coming from me as an ebbing of the energy between us. "We better get you a place to sleep," he said as he got up. "It's getting late, and there's a lot of work to do tomorrow. I'm sure I'll be able to find something to occupy you."

We followed him out of the house to a small building across the lawn, billed as the library. It had sleeping mats on the floor upstairs in a room with sloping ceilings and windows on each gable end that allowed a nice cross breeze. He provided us with blankets, and as he left he turned back toward me.

In a voice imbued with excitement and energy he spoke about my being there and tried to put a positive spin on the event, talking about how it would contribute to the spiritual milieu he envisioned for the farm. I suppose he wanted to make me feel comfortable in the foreign surroundings, but in that attempt he overshot his mark. His words of encouragement combined with his physical position managed to make me feel oddly superior to him. He had paused halfway down the steep set of stairs which had no rails, and thus he only appeared from the chest up in the room in which I stood. I tried to quell my feeling of superiority because on one level I understood it as a foolish interpretation of the situation. I fought the feeling by kneeling on one knee and adopting an exercise which slowed my breathing that I felt would attenuate the surge of power I felt.

After what seemed an interminable time, but in truth probably lasted less than three minutes, Greg finally wished me a good evening and left. My wife lay down on the mats, but I continued in my stance and my effort to quell my emotions through the slowing down of breathing. This practice evolved from a Gurdjieff-inspired effort of emotion control, a Swami Rama understanding of chakras and prana, and my efforts to apply the yoga sutras to ceasing the modifications of my mind.

After a few minutes of slower and slower breathing I finally felt very calm; in fact, I felt strangely too calm. I felt my wrist and could detect no pulse. At that time I didn't realize that some yoga practices taught students how to stop the heart in preparation for leaving the body and performing astral travel. These schools of yoga typically keep the techniques of these practices secret.

In a sense I knelt there all queued up with nowhere to go. Not having expected to have stopped my heart, I felt an unsettled fear. Strangely, though, I did not panic. My pulse did not quicken from a surge of adrenaline. I felt the fear from a distance. Mentally I knew that my body needed my heart to beat, but emotionally I had just put myself in this empty spot where nothing disturbed me.

In a matter-of-fact tone I told my wife, "I have no pulse."

"What?" she spoke in a half-asleep voice.

I repeated myself. "I have no pulse."

I lay back from my kneeling position onto the mat beside her, as she got up on one elbow and put her fingers on my wrist to feel for a pulse.

After a couple of seconds of trying to find a pulse she spurted out, "I'll go get Greg," and she started to get up in a rapid fashion.

"No," I told her. "I want you to stay with me." I pulled on her arm and she stopped getting up.

We embraced for several seconds before she stopped and looked at me with panic in her eyes. Reading the look as a need to do something I instructed her, "Do CPR on me."

"Okay," she agreed. After I lay down flat she pushed down on my chest in a rhythmic fashion with what felt like a ton of pressure. On each stroke I let out a howl. It hurt. After about twenty pushes she stopped. I checked my wrist and then shook my head. I still had no pulse. She did another round of compressions. I howled, except the howls got louder. A second check gave the same result, as did a third. Finally, after the fourth round I pulled her down on me in an embrace. I didn't check for a pulse, but I had enough of the chest compressions. I felt too sore to take any more. I don't know whether she checked for a heartbeat or maybe thought that I had perceived one, but she didn't resist my embrace. We held it for a long time until I fell asleep in her arms.

When I awoke in the morning I found myself alone. I lay on the mat mulling over the previous evening for a while until my wife returned.

"Hi there, how you feeling?" she asked in a cheery greeting as she climbed the stairs

"Where were you?" I responded, ignoring her question.

"I was talking with Greg," she replied. She climbed onto the mat beside me and sat down.

"What did he say about last night?" Before she could answer, I added, "About the noise?" I felt embarrassment from making the loud howls.

"Oh," she laughed, "he just thought you were howling at the moon."

"Oh," I said, puzzled but relieved.

My wife put her hand up to my head and stroked my hair while looking intently at me and smiling. I felt myself relax, but only a small degree. Perhaps I should have taken the cue of her advance, but it never hit me until after a short bit of caressing when she said, "Greg thinks that maybe we should have sex."

Sex could not have been further from my mind. For over six months we hadn't had sexual relations. Ever since my reading of the yoga sutras and taking seriously the recommended practice of sexual continence, I abstained from sex.

"He says that not having sex can cause you to have so much mental energy that you don't know how to handle it. That it can make you unstable," she spoke in a muted voice while she rubbed my shoulders and leaned in to kiss me.

"Oh, is that right?" I responded with a sort of giggle. Bringing up sex had made me feel uncomfortable, not having had it for so long, but she had used such a disarming approach that I felt like a little kid. She kissed my check and stroked my hair. I gave her a hug.

She must have taken the hug as a sign of agreement, or at least interest. "I'm going to slip into, or should I say slip out of, something more comfortable." She turned and walked over to the far side of the room and stepped behind the folding divider screen there. After a few seconds her blouse appeared over the top of the divider.

A feeling of panic rose in me. It had been so long since we had sex that I could not get into the proper frame of mind to end that streak of abstinence. Before she appeared naked before me I snuck down the stairs and out the door. I don't know if she heard me leave, but if she did, she didn't cry after me.

I walked across the road and down a path past an unoccupied farmhouse on the property that led to one of the ponds. The early June morning provided an idyllic setting with birds singing and flowers blooming. Goldfish in the pond came over toward me as I walked along the edge. The path led to a door into the basement at the rear of the house. I tried the door, and when it opened I walked into a shower and bathroom. I hid inside one of the shower stalls for over an hour.

When boredom and hunger finally overtook my aversion to sex, I left the shower and found my way back to the house. Greg, Julie, and Meryl greeted me as though nothing unusual had happened. I ate an orange mostly in silence. When I finished Greg announced we were going to go work in the garden.

We started in the area where the lettuce needed weeding. I worked in one row, Greg in another. In a short time, probably less than twenty minutes, I found my lack of mental focus and physical decline from my weight loss did not promote useful work. My back felt tired. As Greg continued to pull weeds I did some dance-like steps between the rows. Not very graceful or coordinated, but rather jerky and wild.

"What are you doing?" Greg asked when my movements caught his eye.

I didn't answer, but just did another dance step. It felt like what I should do; something inside of me insisted this made sense.

Greg thought otherwise. "Come on, stop that. Let's work," he said.

I did a poorly executed cartwheel.

Greg shook his head and went back to weeding, but it didn't take long before my continued strange actions wore on my host.

He didn't try to argue or plead with me. "Let's go," he said and left the vegetable patch. I followed him toward the house. Inside he put a mellow Hindu chant on the record player. Perhaps he hoped to create a serene atmosphere. Once again I danced. Part of me wanted to impress Greg with the spiritual aspect of my dancing. Somehow it seemed that my movements conveyed something sacred. But Greg ignored my bizarre behavior. At the end of the long-playing record, put out by his indifference to my dancing overtures, I mooned him, then yelled, "You stink," and ran out the front door.

At the time I had no idea why I had said and done such offensive acts. Only much later in my life would those behaviors finally make sense. I did realize at some level that my actions fell into the category of rude behavior. A minute later when I came back into the house, I went up to Greg, offered him my hand and said, "Karma."

"Now we are making progress," Greg replied, as he shook my hand. "Let's go outside."

We went out and sat on the ground in the yard where Greg tried to engage me in talk about a project involving carpentry. Maybe he thought something less boring than weeding could hold my attention.

"We're going to convert the second story over there into sleeping quarters." He pointed to the largest of the buildings across the road.

With my focus still on karma and higher bodies I ignored his reference to the barn across the road and applied his statement in a twisted way to an esoteric view of humans. Gurdjieff referred to the human body as a three-story machine. Eating fed the first story, breathing the second, and ideas the third. Sleeping quarters on the second floor in an obscure confused way meant sleeping while breathing to me. Yogic breathing techniques are call pranayama. I put these thoughts together.

"Sleeping through pranayama?"

"What?" Greg gave me a puzzled look.

I just smiled.

He smiled back at me and shook his head. Then he picked up a small stick and drew in the dirt. "I'm thinking that this will be the layout of the second floor." He sketched several rectangles. "We'll have men sleeping in here." He marked a Y in one rectangle. "And women will stay in these two sections." He scratched two X's.

The XX in the ground morphed into a double helix in my mind. "Self-replication on the second floor." I gave my words a mystical ring and added a flourish of my hands.

Greg gave me a look of disbelief before laughing. His inability to grasp my statements made me feel wiser than him and fueled my efforts to baffle him further.

He made several more attempts to talk about his work on the farm, but they all ended in similar fashion. I kept reading something esoteric into his words and replying with cryptic remarks and odd gestures and movements, each becoming more bizarre and giving me obvious pleasure. Before long Greg stopped seeing anything humorous. He left me by myself.

By this time my wife felt concerned about taking up Greg and Julie's time with my antics. Without my awareness she conferred with Greg about what alternatives might be available for getting my behavior under control. He told her of a nearby medical center that would be able to provide the proper care in a compassionate way. She felt that would be the best move, so he went back in the house and called for an ambulance to come out to the farm.

When the ambulance arrived I had no idea of its purpose. Greg talked with the driver and attendants for a few minutes, and then one of the attendants opened the back while the driver walked over to me and asked, "Do you want to go for a little ride?"

Not the right phrase to use to win my trust. I moved away from the woman who had spoken and replied, "Nobody's going to take me for a ride," with a bit of growl in my voice. Getting taken for a ride held a bad connotation in my mind.

Greg recognized my reaction to the phrase and stepped in. "Nobody's taking you for anything," he said in a gentle tone as he put his hand on my shoulder. Then after a brief pause he pointed to the open ambulance door and said to me, "Come on in here with me."

He walked over to the ambulance and entered through the rear door. Once in, he beckoned for me to follow. The strategy worked. After insulting him earlier, I felt a need to establish trust between us. As soon as I followed him into the back of the ambulance, Greg slipped out through one of the side doors. Meryl entered through the back with me while the attendants quickly secured all exits. The driver took off a second later.

The ambulance picked up speed as it took off down the gravel road, leaving SKY Land behind and spreading a thin veil of dust into the sunlight of the warm spring afternoon. From within the ambulance I waved at Julie and her three-year-old son, and they returned my wave. Greg stood beside them with his hands on his hips, staring past the vehicle into the distance.

# CHAPTER 14

*June 1978, Danville, PA*

The ambulance took us to Geisinger Medical Center in Danville. After a lengthy wait, a nurse brought me and my wife into a narrow room that contained a line of chairs along one side. The nurse told us to have a seat. Then she left the room and returned shortly with a physician. The doctor sat down in the chair adjacent to my wife, with me on the far side. He looked at the clipboard in his left hand.

"Brian, how old are you?"

I found it difficult to make eye contact with the doctor with my wife between us, so before I answered I got up and sat down on the floor to form a triangle between my wife and the doctor. This move seemed entirely appropriate to me, but the doctor, who must have been forewarned about my unusual behavior, felt otherwise.

"Come on, sit in the chair," he said. "Like a normal person."

I didn't appreciate the condescension, since sitting on the floor was "normal" for me. I knew I didn't look like a normal person in my loose-fitting shorts with no socks or shoes and no shirt. I didn't feel normal, either. I was self-conscious about my unusual attire. It had been fine out in the country, but in this modern hospital it really stood out. I chose to make a statement with my position, staking out my identity as different, as much as I chose to avoid craning my neck to talk.

"No," I replied with a smile. "I don't want to upset the circuit-'tree'." With both arms I made a gesture of branches coming up from my sitting position and leading toward the doctor and my wife.

My wife grimaced. "His eating patterns have been rather strange lately," she told him. "I was thinking that maybe he has some kind of dietary imbalance that's causing him to act differently."

The doctor looked askance. "I don't believe a dietary imbalance would have anything to do with bizarre behavior. There is no research that I am aware of that would support this type of conjecture."

"He's been eating a lot of fruit, and I thought maybe he was having a glycemic reaction of some kind."

"Hypoglycemia can cause problems, but it shouldn't result in this kind of behavior."

My wife looked lost. The doctor turned back to me and continued with the series of questions from his clipboard. I found the queries bizarre and inappropriate. They didn't fit my concept of getting to know me and how I was feeling and why. Instead they focused on whether I had a concrete notion of what reality was. "What day of the week is it?" "What year is it?" "What day is your birthday?" "Who is the president of the United States?" the doctor's questioning continued.

"Jimmy Cart..." I paused. "No. Tricky Dick Nixon." I changed my answer and gave a devilish grin. I had enough of the tedious inquiries, and decided to play. What fun is it to answer questions when you know both you and the questioner already know the answers?

The impish side of me gave a few more wacky answers before the interview concluded. In about fifteen minutes my wife and I were escorted to an admissions window. They talked to us, but mostly my wife, as I was not interested in listening. Instead I was engaged in smiling at the people staring at the strange, unshaven, unkempt man in funny-looking shorts. Mostly I was trying to keep my mind clear of negative thoughts about being there.

"Here, honey," my wife prodded. "They want you to sign here."

I gave the paper a distrustful glance. It went against my better judgment to sign something without first reading it.

I shook my head at my wife.

If you are admitted for psychiatric care without signing yourself in—in other words, if you are committed—the law stipulates that a hospital can keep you indefinitely. You can request to be released, but the hospital doesn't have to comply unless you can get a court-ordered release. I didn't understand this at the time, and I only realized that I was being admitted to the hospital when they took me up to the ward and my wife left. This really didn't faze me. I took it without much thought. *So I'm now in my "rubber room,"* I told myself.

I knew that my behavior toward Greg had been strange and that's why I ended up in the "rubber room." I didn't understand why things had happened at the time, but some years later it would make sense.

They never did reveal a diagnosis for my stay. When my wife asked, the attending psychiatrist just said, "We don't like to give these things labels." Label or no label, they absorbed me into the system and began treatment by prescribing me Thorazine, a drug used to treat psychotic behavior. It didn't take long before the dose made concern for my chakras, the ocean of consciousness, and the splitting of my spine fade into oblivion.

When I first arrived in the mental ward I felt self-conscious about being among strangers. The staff eased me into the milieu with an initial twenty-four hours of isolation before they gave me a roommate, introduced me to the daily group therapy sessions, and sent me to what they called occupational therapy, a session that closely resembled the arts and crafts time at Bible School I had experienced as a kid. These gatherings at first bored me and made me feel patronized, but after the third day I began participating to break the monotony and to let them see me behaving in a way that I supposed they would see as normal, but to me simply seemed childish. I mean, *geesh*, when does someone rave over a thirty-year-old making a cardboard model of a pyramid? But, yes indeed, they did just that when my boredom led me to construct one.

By the end of day seven I felt anxious to leave. By then I felt at ease with most of the people, but the mediocre food, lack of privacy, and sparse contact with Meryl made the place uninviting. Fortunately, on day nine of my stay a breakthrough occurred. Chuck, a social worker, talked about his love of ping-pong. I played a pretty good game while at college, so I challenged him to a match. He accepted and we headed off to the rec room.

After warming up for several minutes we started keeping score. I fell behind early, but bore down and came from behind to win by the smallest of margins.

"You're pretty good," he said.

"Thanks. I haven't played for a while, but it comes back to you."

"Yes, you picked it up in the second half. Do you want to play some more?"

My heart was pounding and my knees felt weak. "I don't think so. These meds that I'm taking made it pretty difficult." I'd needed extra adrenaline to win and now my legs felt like jelly.

"Okay. I said I would play a game, not that we would play until I beat you. Maybe next time."

"I don't think there will be a next time. I intend to leave tomorrow." For a couple of days I had considered asking to be discharged. The ping-pong victory boosted my confidence and I decided to make my move.

Chuck looked surprised. "Oh? Dr. Houser didn't say anything to me."

Dr. Houser was my psychiatrist. "No. I didn't say anything to anyone before. I'm just now telling you."

Chuck knew the situation. He knew that I needed the hospital to approve my leaving without a court injunction. "Okay. I'll let him know your plans."

Later that day they called me to Dr. Houser's office. "So what about feeling like your spine is splitting and going over to the ocean of consciousness?" he asked.

"I really haven't thought much about that since the first day here. I guess I put it on the back burner somewhere." Although my foray into the world of chakras and prana had captivated me, it hadn't made me lose sight of reality. I knew the score. If I kept thinking and saying crazy things, I wouldn't be getting out. The Thorazine made it easy to comply with this necessity.

The doctor asked a few more general questions about my plans for the future. He knew I had a good relationship with my wife, and my father had visited and showed his concern and support. My request to leave seemed reasonable to him. "Sometimes the patient lets us know when it is time."

Dr. Houser advised me that I would need to take the strong antipsychotic drug he prescribed for at least two years. However, once Meryl and I moved in with my father and younger sister for the summer two weeks after leaving the hospital, I quit taking the medicine and felt much better upon stopping. Without the social isolation, my strange breathing exercises, and radical diet, my behavior was fine without medication. I started eating cooked food again and gained back twenty-five pounds of weight in only a few months.

*August 1978, Williamsport, PA*

At the beginning of the school year we moved to the city of Williamsport, close to where Meryl taught, and I completed my reintegration into society. I enrolled in a correspondence course in electronics and visited the public library almost every day. I returned to SKY Land in the spring of the following year to attend a weekend yoga conference to the astonishment of Greg.

"People who go off the deep end in their yoga practices almost never go back to practicing yoga at all," Greg told me.

When I'd found myself in the deep end I hadn't sunk into despair. Instead I learned to swim to where I could stand on my own. I was determined to continue my spiritual quest, but I learned a lesson about working by myself. I would proceed within the context of a tested path, at least for now. I intended to limit my spiritual practices to those sanctioned by living, in-the-flesh teachers and not to isolate myself from society.

Over the next year I bought an oscilloscope and a soldering iron, along with a couple of electronic kits to assemble, and completed the correspondence course. With this modest background, I found a decent job as an electronics technician.

An even bigger change came into my life after I gave up celibacy and became a father. Meryl didn't return to teaching after her maternity leave, but left the bread winning to me and took up child rearing. The addition of a child did not impede my desire to study yoga. In fact, Meryl and I practiced yoga together, and our interest in this ancient philosophy grew to a point that we spent over a half hour a day doing yoga and meditating.

When our son, Aaron, reached eighteen months old, we decided to enroll together in a weekend yoga retreat at the ashram of yogi Amrit Desai. Meryl and I heard about Desai's reputation for generating positive spiritual change and we wanted to investigate his system of yoga. We dropped our boy off at his grandparents' and made the two-hour drive in high anticipation.

# Chapter 15

*October 1980, Rural Berks County, PA*

The Kripalu Ashram had the appearance of a small college campus, while its isolated location enhanced its quaint beauty and added a spiritual flavor. Meryl and I arrived in the early evening and parked in the large visitor's lot situated on the western edge of the dozen buildings that comprised the center. As we got out of the car and stretched, the smell of fall leaves added to the sensual impact of the beautiful architecture. It felt as though we found a refuge from the madness of our society's fast-paced culture.

We oriented ourselves using the pre-registration map and then proceeded to the center's main building, a large stucco structure in the Spanish style of the southwest with sweeping arches leading onto an open portico that led halfway around the building. The plainness of the adobe sides stood in contrast to the twin eight-foot hand-carved oak doors. The doors seemed a bit formal and foreboding, hardly a place where one would find an introductory anything. We stood still in front of the doors for a second before I opened them with caution. From the brochure I knew this was a public building, but I felt like an intruder.

Inside the great doors a vestibule held dozens of cubby holes on both sides, and a sign reading, "Please remove your shoes." Meryl and I placed our shoes together in one of the empty holes, and walked into the main foyer. There we took our place at the end of a line of guests queued up in front of a long reception table. Three women sat behind it helping people register and handing out name tags. Each of these women wore a long, loose, white cotton dress and a colorful scarf or hair bow. Several others, men in white pants and white shirts and more women dressed like the others, shuffled business-like about the spacious entry room, accommodating guests and their belongings. As we waited in line the initial feeling of being part of the "out" crowd, by virtue of our non-white attire, melted away thanks to the genuine friendliness and lack of self-consciousness of the white-clad ashram residents.

"The men will be sleeping on the floor of the main chapel area. Since we'll be using that space for a gathering in just a short while, you can keep your bedding and things in the dressing room through those doors," one of the receptionists told me with a smile as I handed her my pre-registration form.

The woman turned to Meryl and said, "The women will be sleeping in the men's building. The men have vacated for the weekend." She pointed to the men's quarters on a map of the campus. Then she handed us our name tags and said, "The evening program starts in the main chapel, through those doors, in about half an hour." She pointed to a large open entrance on her left.

For the next twenty minutes we strolled about the campus, inhaling the fall air and acquainting ourselves with the ashram as we relaxed from the drive. When we returned to the main building, a large crowd of maybe one hundred guests and thirty residents filled the main hall. The residents all wore white and gathered in the front right section of the room where the noise from their laughter and conversations stood in contrast to the quiet guests spread more sparsely throughout the rest of the room.

A large, over-stuffed red chair located on a low stage in the middle at the front provided the room's only furniture. Behind the chair hung a large picture of an elderly man dressed in white. To the left of the chair two musical instruments rested on the floor, a portable harmonium, an electronic keyboard the size of an accordion, and a tabla, a set of two small drums. The residents and most of the guests sat cross-legged on the floor. A few folks stood in the back and leaned against the walls, looking uncomfortable in the seatless environment. We sat beside some other guests and crossed our legs in our accustomed meditation poses. The thick carpet felt comfortable on our shoeless feet and the acoustic tiles on the ceiling and walls provided a hushed atmosphere in the back half of the room where we sat.

In a short while, a petite woman dressed in white with a few flowers in her hair walked to the front and picked up a microphone that had been draped over the chair. "May I have your attention please? Yogi Desai will be with us shortly, but first we'd like you to join us, if you will, in some singing."

She clipped the microphone to the collar of her dress and sat down on the floor to the left of the chair. Then she put the small keyboard on her lap and played a few chords by pressing buttons on the side of the device with her left hand. An organ-like sound came through the numerous speakers embedded in the ceiling. "Every night we hold a session where we all get together for a talk from Gurudev."

She played more chords and then added single notes using her right hand on the keyboard. "Gurudev, that's what we call yogi Desai," she continued playing and talking. "But before he comes we always sing some Bhajans, traditional Hindu chants."

She increased the volume on her instrument and continued playing. "These are simple songs. Everyone can help. All you have to do is repeat each phrase after me."

While she spoke, a slender, young male with short, dark hair walked onto the elevated area. With one graceful movement he picked up the tabla and sat down.

The notes from the harmonium took the form of a melody. "Just listen to the others," the woman said above the music, and then after a few more bars added, "Oh, if we start clapping and dancing don't be alarmed. We're all pretty uninhibited."

Laughter came from the disciples of the yogi.

"Feel free to join," she said.

The woman now sang along with her music the words of a traditional Hindu religious song. It started out slowly with only the sweet sound of her instrument accompanying her. She sang a phrase and the other disciples sang it back to her. As the song progressed the phrases stayed the same or only changed slightly, however, the tempo gradually increased.

Soon some of the guests joined with the disciples. As the tempo increased even more, the percussionist added a rhythm with the tabla. At this point the disciples got up and danced or swayed to the music and clapped. The beat continued to get faster, and soon half the crowd stood on its feet clapping and moving to the music and singing loudly, including me. It felt good to get up and move, and the friendliness of the residents had made me feel accepted and part of the group. After the tempo could not be increased or sustained any longer the singing finally came to an abrupt close.

The leader took a few breaths, and then told everyone, "That was good. I'm glad to see so many of you help." She played a few slow notes. "Let's try another."

The notes again turned into a melody and she chanted new lyrics. The others joined in as before and the same progression took place. Slow singing, faster singing, percussion, dancing, clapping, fast singing, faster singing, climax, done.

A few seconds after the second song finished the vocalist spoke. "We like to do this," she said with her eyes closed, "every night." A few notes sounded. "It gets us in the proper spirit for Gurudev." She played slow notes for almost a minute, all the time keeping her eyes closed. "Yogi Desai will be here very shortly now," she promised. The notes on the keyboard formed a melody once again.

I smiled when I heard the first words of the third chant. The first two had lifted me into an altered state. I felt almost as though I could float across the room. I whispered to my wife, "This chanting has an intoxicating effect." I didn't get any response, only a grin.

The chanting continued, following the pattern of the previous two, but before the tempo reached a climax a young male entered the room through the rear doors with a conch shell in his hands. He put the shell to his mouth and blew.

*Brrrrrrrut! Brrrrrrrut! Brrrrrrrut!*

The music halted. All of the residents stopped dancing and turned to face the main entrance at the back. Two men held open the doors and through them walked a man in a white robe, hands pressed together tightly to his chest in prayer position. The white-clad followers of Desai faced the man with hands placed in this position, too.

The holy man walked at a slow pace down the aisle through the middle of the room toward his waiting chair. He carried himself with a regal air, but at the same time with meekness in his visage.

He prostrated himself on the floor beneath the portrait on the wall, a picture of his guru, and recited a Sanskrit phrase in a loud voice. The disciples in the room also bowed down and repeated the same devotional phrase. With the opening ceremonial show of deference to his teacher completed, the yogi got up and turned to face the group. In a graceful movement he took flowers from behind his ear and threw them toward the disciples. A number of squeals greeted the floating flowers as the female members grabbed them. Then without any apparent effort the yogi situated himself cross-legged on his plush seat. The female who had led the songs helped him attach the lapel microphone before she took a seat in front with the other disciples who also sat down.

He spoke in a deliberate manner with a strong Hindi accent. "It's good to see all of you here tonight, and to hear all of your voices," he said. "Did you have enough chanting?"

A few loud protests from the disciples sifted through the air.

The yogi was already reaching for the keyboard. He gave a small laugh. "You never have enough chanting until you are truly enchanted." He played a new tune in the style of the others.

The chanting seemed even more intense than before with a strong male voice leading. After that tune finished and another, the energy level of the voices finally subsided and the yogi put the instrument away. The chanting lasted over thirty minutes, and although I didn't understand a word, or perhaps because I didn't understand a word, my spirit soared. None of my previous experiences with chanting had ever reached such a level, but I didn't have time to revel in the giddy state. The yogi brought everyone back to earth with his intense, accented English.

"Now you are warmed up," the leader said. A big toothy smile appeared on his face. "How do you like it so far?" he asked. His eyes twinkled. "Do you feel a little uncomfortable? No shoes. Sitting on the floor." He kept grinning. "What about the way everybody bowed down? And when I threw the flowers to the group?" A look of mock dismay appeared on his face. "They seem to worship me. Isn't that terrible? Isn't that evil? The way I have control over these helpless people." Mock astonishment and dismay. "Oh, no!"

He paused and the mock look of despair dissipated, replaced by a genuine smile. "What you have to realize in order to understand all of these things is that they are all traditions. Customs brought from my homeland. My country is very tradition oriented. It's not like here where everything is new. Where you use something a while then discard it. Throw it away and find something different."

He paused before continuing in his slow, even rate. "In India, my country, things and ideas are kept and cherished and valued. And not for any other reason than that's the way it's been. It's a very non-rationalistic society. We don't rationalize our every act the way people do over here." He paused as he switched to his mock mode. "Oh, I think I'll make this new recipe I just found for dinner tonight. It's part of a diet that's supposed to lose all my fat. Hmm, maybe I'll go to the movies. The one showing is supposed to be very good for raising your social consciousness. Or maybe I'll start doing yoga. I've read that it's very good for the spine." A big grin appeared on his face as many in the audience self-consciously laughed.

He paused as he looked around the room and then resumed. "Indian people's diets and social behavior are not rationalized about. They happen in a very different way, a very emotive way. The emotion of tradition. Don't misunderstand what I'm saying, now. I'm not trying to say your culture is all bad and mine all good. What I'm trying to point out here is the different modes of thought underlying or at the basis of the different cultures. Yours is a very rational, very left-brain culture. India's is emotive, right-brained. What would be best is where right brain and left brain thinking would be present in equal amounts." He paused again, as if to let his ideas have enough time to sink in.

"That's what yoga is all about," he continued. "Balance. No yoga exercise is complete without symmetry, without balance. If you do something to one side of the body, you have to do it to the other. If you bend one way, you have to bend the opposite way." He accentuated his slow articulation with graceful hand gestures. "And it should be the same way with our minds if we want to be in harmony, in union, in yoga. If we operate rationally all the time we get very much out of balance. We need that right-brain experience to even things out. That's what I hope this weekend can do for you. Give you that emotive experience. Something you can't sit down and rationalize about. That kind of experience is very much needed in this culture at this time. As I said, people in your country rationalize almost every move. It's unhealthy being so much out of balance. It has got to the point where people start rationalizing about whether they should have a right-brain experience."

He paused for the giggles coming from the right front section. Then he continued, "They become afraid, paranoid about becoming irrational. Scared that they might do something without a reason or understanding."

He switched to jesting again, "Oh, I don't want to go to that yoga retreat. Something might happen there that I won't understand. There might be something I can't explain. I better stay away."

A few nervous giggles could be heard, this time from the guests in the audience. "But don't be afraid," he sounded sincere and innocent. "I'm not going to hurt you. No one's going to take your free will. Open up. Use a new part of your mind. Become aware of the possibilities of right-brain thinking... of the beauties associated with emotion... of feeling. Don't look at all of these new things with fear. Look at them as beautiful expressions of emotion."

A longer than usual pause ensued as he seemed to be gauging his audience's reaction. Then he continued, "Maybe you are worried about how these people treat me. How they revere me. Perhaps some of you are thinking, 'Oh, this is very pretty, but I could never let myself do that. Worship someone!' But let me tell you that I didn't decide to become a guru. It didn't happen that one day I said, 'Oh, I think I'll become a guru now'."

Giggles arose from his group of followers in response to his self-ridicule.

"'That would be nice. I'd have a lot of people bow down at my feet. Yes, that would be fun.'" Another long pause and big grin. "No, that's not how it happened. What happened is that people started to perceive me differently. The students I taught stopped seeing me merely as an instructor, someone who tells you how to do an exercise the correct way. They noticed something different in my spirit. My countenance became brighter. A force of some kind was working through me. The Bible says there will be other prophets that will be called sons of God."

He hesitated at this point, realizing he had made a serious, almost ominous pronouncement. Then in an effort to lighten the mood, he added, "And by their fruits you shall know them. Just look around you. You see all these people dressed in white? These are my fruits." The remark evoked loud laughter throughout the room.

With a smile he waited for silence, and then continued in a different tone, "I'd like to open up the discussion to members of the group. Please ask questions you might have about our ashram and what we do here."

Several guests raised their hands. One of the disciples walked over to where the tabla player sat, took the microphone used for the tabla, and walked into the audience to a male guest with a raised hand. The man spoke into the microphone. "You said a force of some kind was working through you. Could you tell us more about that force?"

Desai replied, "What was this force that people saw in me? What made me seem to be brighter to them? No one really knows for sure. Nobody can really define it. It's a mystery. That's where the word mysticism comes from, the mysterious force that manifests itself through certain holy men. Where did it come from? It's been around since recorded history. How does it get passed down? Through the guru. My guru," he gestured toward the picture behind him, "has passed this power on to me."

Desai paused and the guest asked, "How did your guru transfer this force?"

The holy man replied, "Through a process we know as shaktiput. Shaktiput can take place through touching or just looking. Do you remember the story in the New Testament where Christ asked 'Who touched me?'"

"Yes," the questioner replied. "Does that mean the disciple can initiate this transfer?"

"It's possible, but it doesn't happen without the knowledge or consent of the guru. In India the guru is always responsible for shaktiput. It's our system of respect. Perhaps Christ was so open that he allowed the transfer of energy freely without demanding the respect that our system has built in."

The first questioner gave the microphone back to the disciple, who then handed it to a female guest. "Do you have the power to administer shaktiput?" she asked.

"Yes, to a degree, to a certain level," he answered.

"What are the levels?" the same guest continued.

"It's not easy to describe the levels briefly. If you are interested in learning more details about shaktiput there is a book on the subject in our bookstore upstairs."

The microphone was handed to another member of the audience. "Why does the Indian yoga system demand such respect to the point of practically worshiping the leader?"

"That is not an easy question for Westerners to understand. Yet it seems so simple to those of us who have lived with this system all of our lives."

The guru's answer continued, but I lost interest. The questions bored me. They had a press conference atmosphere. The spontaneous statement delivered by the guru had fascinated me, but the questions came from sources without the power and assurance of the leader. To me some of the questioners seemed like vultures wanting to tear him apart and then pick his bones to grab any morsel he might hold. Others seemed more like beggars who'd like a crust if he'd just throw one their direction.

I blocked out the proceedings and slipped into a meditative state, trying to recall the ecstatic feeling the chanting had given me. I ignored the questions and answers by not registering or processing the contents of the spoken words. I kept my eyes open on the guru, and tried to view the yogi on a non-rational basis and not analyze him. I wanted to give my right brain a chance like Desai had encouraged the group to do.

As I sat concentrating on this effort I suddenly felt a warm sensation in my heart chakra, the center of my chest. Along with this came a realization of an emotional bond between myself and the yogi, and an indescribable spiritual feeling. I showed no reaction to my experience, but just sat in a more or less grateful daze during the duration of the questioning.

As the questions tapered off, the guru advised the group to retire early. It was already 9:15 and the day's routine started at 4:30 A.M. The guru closed the evening's activities with the same ritual he had started with, a bow to the portrait and a Sanskrit prayer. The disciples did the same. Afterwards the ashram leader walked back through the divided crowd to the rear exit of the room where he waited, hands in prayer position, while a young disciple put sandals on the guru's feet.

I sat still for a long while after the yogi had left, not wanting to lose the feeling from the experience. As the crowd filed out, those around me saw that I didn't want to be disturbed and left me alone. After the last of the crowd left I finally got up.

"I really enjoyed the chanting and I liked his little talk," I told my wife. "I like his sense of humor. This place does have a real charm. Everything's so different from what we normally experience in our culture."

"Yes, and it's not a fake atmosphere," Meryl said. "Everyone seems so genuine." As she spoke we noticed several men already spreading out their sleeping bags in the room. It seemed like a hint for the women to clear out.

"If we're going to get up in less than seven hours, maybe I need to head off to my sleeping quarters and get settled in," she said. Then she added, "At least, I need to get out of here."

A fresh, cool evening breeze welcomed us as we walked out of the main building. With all the people moving about after the evening program, the ashram grounds looked like a college campus at the time of classes changing, except everyone whispered. We stopped at the walkway leading to the entrance of the women's quarters and I gave Meryl a gentle kiss goodnight on the forehead. "I feel like I'm on a date," she said.

"Yeah, I know what you mean. Feels funny saying goodnight this way, like we did back in college," I told her. I gave her a wink and started back toward the larger building.

# CHAPTER 16

*October 1980, Rural Berks County, PA*

The next day gave us a taste of ashram life: up at 4:30 to go for a jog, yoga class at 6:00 that tested my endurance, and stretching capabilities before a light breakfast. In the morning program Yogi Desai put on a demonstration of yoga postures. His tall, supple body moved through many difficult poses with ease and grace. Afterwards he offered some mantras before taking questions and comments about individual experiences. When the yogi finished and left through a side entrance, an aide spoke from the front.

"That concludes this morning's program. The next scheduled event for the weekend is lunch, served at noon in the cafeteria on the second floor."

People headed for the exit at the rear of the room.

After a short pause the young woman continued, "Some people have asked about becoming a disciple of Gurudev. If anyone is interested in joining the Kripalu community, Gurudev would like to say a few words to you. Please come to the front and Yogi Desai will come to speak with you in a few minutes." She said this as if it were an afterthought rather than an advertisement. Instead of trying to lure folks into the ashram it seemed more like she had a reluctance to invite us. More like an *"Okay, I guess I have to ask you guys"* than a *"Please come join us."*

About a half dozen people gathered in the front of the room with the woman who had offered the invitation. Although she was not enthusiastic about the idea, I cajoled my wife into joining the group. In a few minutes the guru reappeared.

"First, I would like to commend everyone for being open-minded enough to consider joining the Kripalu community." He spoke in a somber tone, compared to the much more upbeat approach he had used earlier. "I know that anybody thinking about such a move has to weigh many factors. I'm sure you have questions concerning life here that you would like to ask, but before you do I would like Darmisha to give you her view of life at the ashram."

"Thank you, Gurudev." She nodded to her teacher and then turned toward the group.

"We have a regimented way of life here, very disciplined. Everyone is expected to adhere to a strict schedule. We think it promotes a feeling of unity among the residents, a feeling of family. We don't allow individuals to 'do their own thing', like many of you are accustomed to.

"We arise early every morning, at 4:30. Our day starts with individual practices of meditation and yoga. Some people go running at that time. These activities last until 6:00, when we gather for a group session where somebody leads in yoga postures and breathing exercises. We finish with chanting. We eat our breakfast together at 6:30. Then we have individual duties until the evening meal. Many of us work outside the ashram. Others have specific functions in the ashram and our new holistic health center. Everyone is expected to contribute service time that promotes the general welfare of the ashram on their days off.

"In the evenings we look forward to talks from Gurudev, if he is here. He usually spends four or five days a week here and two or three days a week in the smaller facility in Sumneytown. If Gurudev is not here, another person leads the evening program where we do more chanting.

"That gives you a pretty good idea of life here." Darmisha turned to Desai. "Guruji, do you want to add anything?"

"Do any of you have a question about living here that you would like to ask either of us?"

A young woman asked in a meek tone, "What about pets? I have a small dog."

"I'm sorry, we don't allow any pets," Darmisha replied.

The woman tried to plead her case by getting teary eyed, but the rules did not bend. It seemed obvious that the folks running Kripalu did not want to paint a rosy picture of an easy life at the ashram. Instead they presented a picture of a tightly run operation, where slacking and rule-bending had no place.

Another question concerned room and board. How much? Could a resident work to pay for it? The cost wasn't cheap, but not outrageous. They did have people who worked for room and board, but no current openings. The construction season was winding down and men who had been building outside would soon have their work curtailed. They offered a limited number of scholarships.

"What about married couples?" I asked.

"We don't have married couples at this location, other than the physician who works at the holistic health center. We don't have individual rooms for couples. All the men here live in one living unit and the women live together in another, separate unit. There are some married couples at the Sumneytown location, though."

The session ended after only a few more simple questions. Afterwards I took a long walk with my wife to talk about joining the ashram. I can't say that Meryl had much enthusiasm for the idea, although she did see my interest. We agreed to visit the Sumneytown ashram soon to get a feel for it and see if we might find it a suitable place to live and grow.

The weekend continued with more chanting that evening and more yoga the next morning. It took my spirits even higher than before. I wanted to embrace this spirit I felt. I felt ready for full immersion.

# Chapter 17

*November 1980, Sumneytown, PA*

Two weeks after the yoga retreat we traveled with our son for an overnight visit to the other Kripalu facility. After a long, nerve-fraying drive through Friday evening urban traffic, we found the small campus along a busy road in the outer suburbs of Philadelphia. Unlike the Summit Station location, the Sumneytown ashram did not feel like an escape from the rush of modern life.

I parked the car and donned a light jacket to ward off the coolness of the late autumn evening before taking Aaron out of his car seat.

"Which building do we go to?" I asked my wife. In the shadows of the lights from the parking lot I saw three structures that appeared to comprise the complex.

"I don't know. The person I talked to when I made the arrangements said to go into the main building and just talk to anyone and tell them why you've come. Apparently they get visitors on a regular basis, so everyone knows what's supposed to happen."

None of the buildings had any signs. "So which is the main building?"

Meryl shrugged. "Pick one."

A path off to the left led up some steps to the back door of an older house the size of a residence. On the right stood a much larger, newer brick structure, perhaps a set of apartments. It didn't have any entrance facing the lot. The building at the far end of the parking area, a large white house, had a walkway with steps leading to what looked like a main doorway. I headed toward it.

"Let's try this one."

When we reached the porch I stood holding my son for a moment, wondering whether to knock or just enter. "Better knock," I muttered, not feeling like I was in the right place.

A young male in his late twenties answered the door. "You want something?" he asked with a bewildered look, as he pulled a gray sweatshirt over his head.

"Is this the Kripalu Ashram?"

The man straightened the sleeves of his sweatshirt and shook his head to get his long blond hair out of his eyes. He looked from me to my son and then to my wife and back at me before saying, "Yeah, it is."

From his apprehensive demeanor I could tell something wasn't right. "Well, uh," I stammered. "We made arrangements to visit here."

"This is the male living quarters," he said, as if I should have known. "You probably want to go over there." He pointed toward the apartment building.

I looked to see where he pointed and then turned back to thank him, but the door was already shut.

We walked through the parking lot and part-way back down the entrance driveway in order to find the door to the "main" building. Once inside, we walked through the downstairs corridor but found no one. We passed door after door of what looked like the inside of a motel rather than an apartment building. Then we walked up the stairs and down the deserted second-floor hallway, past another row of doors. As we headed back to the stairs, a woman appeared at one of the doors.

Jeanne introduced herself, and when she learned why we had come she set us up in one of the vacant apartments. Our "apartment" consisted of a single small room, a typical living space for married residents, Jeanne informed us. She also told us that all of the rooms had little furniture, usually just a dresser for clothing, and sometimes a small altar. No beds. Everyone slept on the floor on mats.

"How many folks live at the ashram?" I asked Jeanne after she provided us with a set of linens.

"There are about two dozen unmarried men in the other unit and about a dozen unmarried women here in this building, along with six married couples."

"Any children?"

"Just my daughter."

"How is it, raising your girl here?"

The woman looked down and didn't respond right away. "It's difficult," she said in a slow, detached way.

We could hear the tension in her voice. Then she looked up and changed the subject and brightened her tone.

"Tonight's program will start in a half hour over in our gathering place, directly across the parking lot from here. Did you eat before you arrived?"

"Yes," Meryl responded. "They told us when the evening meal would be and we knew we couldn't make it in time."

"Well, I'll see you in a half hour."

The evening's event took place in a modest-sized room that looked like it had once been two rooms, maybe a dining room and a living room. A small stage at one end held a harmonium and tabla. The space would have been packed if all fifty residents of the ashram would have come, but less than two dozen people, mostly women, showed. As we waited in uncomfortable silence for the program to start, no one spoke to us. I couldn't figure out why nobody wanted to know who we were or why no one welcomed us. Was it part of the rigid protocol?

With Yogi Desai at Summit Station, one of the older disciples led the meeting. The chanting began as it had at the weekend retreat. Slow music and singing at first, then as the speed and intensity increased folks danced and swayed to the beat. I joined them, but Meryl had to keep holding our son, whose restlessness escalated as soon as everyone started dancing. By the second number she had to leave the room with our fussy child.

I stayed and tried to revel in the moment, but without my partner beside me I felt uncomfortable. The woman directly in front of me created a distraction I tried hard to ignore, but failed to do so. She wore the standard white cotton outfit, a loose top, but not loose enough pants. Her athletic hips and plump buttocks filled out the seat of her attire and she waved her booty with great gusto to the beat, providing a view that I might have enjoyed if I had an interest in seeking her sexual favors. However, with my aim of achieving a higher state of consciousness, her gyrations only caused me anguish.

After the leader closed the meeting I rejoined Meryl back at our room. We spoke a few words with a childless married couple before retiring for the evening. Their assessment of life at the ashram also pointed to hardships and struggles to remain dedicated. I was hoping for more enthusiasm.

The next morning we left early. I felt like a dog with his tail tucked between his legs. Meryl and I needed less than a minute to discuss the possibility of living there. Although I felt that the ashram could engender my own personal spiritual growth, we both agreed that our family would not thrive. My family's well-being came first. My dream of finding a teacher had to continue elsewhere.

# Chapter 18

*November 1980, Carlisle, PA*

After the powerful emotional experience with the Hindu Bhajans at Kripalu, I added chanting to my daily yoga practices, but I wasn't satisfied to simply chant the traditional mantras without knowing anything about the process. I wanted to understand how sounds could have an emotional impact. What particular sounds had what specific effects?

I spent considerable time each day for several days working with individual sounds and how the shape of the mouth and the position of the tongue and jaw changed from sound to sound, and what emotion I felt when expressing a particular sound.

One evening after twenty minutes of sitting cross-legged in the middle of the room and trying to feel the precise effects of each sound that I uttered, I grew tired. I straightened my legs, pushed myself back against the nearby wall, and closed my eyes.

In my meditation practices I often experienced visualizations. Sometimes when I would close my eyes, images would come into view for a brief period. The images most often consisted of unidentifiable blurs of lights. Sometimes a recognizable object would appear, but these always faded quickly or morphed into something indistinguishable. These, I surmised, all had something to do with the way the neurons spontaneously fired in my occipital cortex when I deprived them of input by closing my eyes. To some degree I learned how to control these neuron firings by controlling my thoughts, thus making them somewhat less spontaneous, but these efforts never resulted in me seeing something I could mistake for reality.

What happened on this day as I leaned back and closed my eyes did not compare to my earlier visualizations. This day I had what I call a "vision." A psychologist might categorize the event as lucid dreaming—dreaming while remaining fully conscious. Although this might explain the experience best from the pantheon of terms available to us at this point in our development of the science of psychology, this does not satisfy me. It would mean that I went from wide awake to dreaming in less than one second.

When I closed my eyes I saw a lush field as clearly as if I stood in one. Or rather, as if I hovered above one, as my perspective did not include my body. I did see things from a normal standing height, though. The abrupt change of perspective from my room to an unrecognizable field startled me, but I didn't try to understand it or reason about it. Instead I reacted as though I did stand in this field, even though I had no awareness of a physical presence.

I appraised the field, looking around to evaluate possible options for interacting with this new environment. After only a few moments of shifting my visual field I noticed some people sitting by a stream maybe a hundred yards away to the right. With my curiosity piqued, I felt an urge to explore and learn more about these folks. Immediately my awareness floated toward them without any physical effort, in a slow, gentle motion.

As I came closer I could identify three men, all dressed in traditional Arab garb. They sat crossed-legged around an object centered between them. At first I could not identify the object, but I could see that each of the men stared directly at it, as if captivated. As I sought to understand what held their attention my awareness drew closer.

When my gaze came within a few yards, it struck me that the object looked like a roulette wheel, and I wondered if they were gambling. But as I pondered that issue, I floated directly over the object and saw its true identity—an immense, shimmering quartz crystal. In a fraction of a second my awareness plunged into the stone and an overwhelming feeling of awe overtook me. It seemed as though the light that reflected through the clear gemstone pierced my being and filled my heart chakra with a timeless, unconditional love. I luxuriated in this feeling for an unknown period before I opened my eyes and found myself sitting in my apartment room pondering the meaning of the vision. I didn't have long to wait for an answer to that puzzle.

That evening my wife arrived home and announced, "This book almost jumped off the shelf at me," as she handed me a copy of Pir Vilayet Inyat Khan's *Toward the One*. I opened the book and saw a Sufi dressed like the men in the vision. My wife's psychic ability to feed my mind had come through again.

For the next month I devoured the book and learned about the Sufis, a centuries old mystical group within Islam. The work had many themes and goals, but the most striking one to me centered on the use of sound. Pir Vilayet had presented work that fit with my efforts to understand how individual sounds impacted particular emotions. My excitement in reading these pages grew daily. A framework for sounds and emotions took on a nascent outline. An interpretation of the three men in the vision started to make sense. In my practice with chanting sounds, I could identify three primary vowel sounds. It paralleled the established concept that human perception of all colors is based upon three primary colors.

After finishing the book I reread the parts about sounds for a second and a third time until I felt empty. How could that fantastic ride through new understandings just end? How could I expand my knowledge of this? I wondered whether anyone in the West had undertaken research on these matters.

I felt unsure about exploring this avenue, having forsaken Western thinking for the past several years in favor of the teachings of Gurdjieff and Patanjali's yoga sutras. These sources of understanding and pursuit of enlightenment took an approach opposite to that of Western science. Part of me didn't trust what some with a solely empirical bent would pronounce on the things that I held dear, but another part of me, my rational part, wanted to know more about sounds and how they affected emotions.

With trepidation I visited the local public library. I didn't want to keep denying Western science. I wanted to embrace it, to see it expand and bring light to the subject, but I dreaded what I would find. I feared it would end the excitement I felt about the discovery of my new knowledge.

Once I reached the library it took me some time to locate the stacks with books on language. I hadn't spent much time in a library for years. The last time I had visited one I had lived in another city. This was my first trip to this building. Once I found the right section for books on language, a book seemed to hop out at me with a glowing energy as I pulled it from the shelf. My attention focused on *The Story of Language* by Mario Pei.

I opened the book and flipped through the pages with a sense of urgency. I noticed a section on vowels and read the passage. To my astonishment the text said that every language had at least the same three basic vowels, the same three that I had identified through self-study as primary. The book stated that if the language had additional vowels then all other vowels consisted of parts of the three basic ones. Proof of my theory of three primary vowels lay right in front of me.

I felt an overwhelming surge of joy. I practically sprang up from my squatting position and walked out of the stacks. As I walked, no inner dialogue went on inside my head. Often I had tried to attain such a state, but I never achieved this much success. Years before I tried to "stop the inner dialogue" while walking the fields and forests of central PA, just as Don Juan had urged Carlos Castaneda. My efforts for ceasing the modifications of my mind in recent years happened with my eyes closed in meditation, where lack of sensory distractions made it somewhat easier. But now I walked down the stairs to the main floor of the library without any reflections, without any thoughts racing, or even plodding through my mind. I just felt a satisfying peace. I didn't ponder the significance of my clear mind, but rather reveled in it.

In this clear state I walked into a section of the library that I hadn't visited yet. It was the reference section, although I didn't realize its function at the time. I felt as though an autopilot feature had taken over my motor control. I didn't think about it or worry about it, though. I felt totally in control of myself. I had a quiet inner calm. I just watched as I pulled out a book without noticing the title was *Peterson's Guide to Graduate Schools*.

I leafed through the pages, oblivious to the contents, not trying to read or figure anything out. After a short bit of thumbing though the book, I quit paging and my fingers ran down the left side of the opened page and came to a halt. I froze. No more movement. At this point I surmised that I should begin to read where my finger pointed.

I read "Tufts University Graduate School of Psychology." The universe had just given me a direction.

# CHAPTER 19

*March 1981, Rural Perry County, PA*

"You can come out to live with us if you like," my uncle told me. "We have room in our home for you and your family while you find a job and a place to live. The opportunities for someone with your background are unlimited there." My uncle, a successful CEO of a high-tech firm in Silicon Valley, was in Pennsylvania for the funeral of his mother, my grandmother.

"That's very generous of you," I said, replying to his offer that came after I had told him about my job and experience as an electronics technician. The conversation soon shifted to other topics, but this offer stuck in my mind.

After the experience in the library I anguished over my prospects for getting into Tufts University Graduate School. Since I had not yet finished a bachelor's degree, the possibility of graduate school seemed remote. I didn't see an easy path to it. Certainly staying at my job as an electronics technician wouldn't get me there, and getting those nine credits I needed for my bachelor's seemed out of reach. I had one child and a second on the way. The financial responsibilities of parenthood weighed upon me.

But a few weeks later I saw a way out of my current position. I learned that the Omega Institute offered a three-day course featuring spiritual leaders from Christian, Jewish, Buddhist, Hindu, and Muslim spiritual traditions. Pir Vilayat—the leader of the Sufi Order of the West and the author of the book on sounds that had electrified me—would be there to present his viewpoint.

I quit my job before the Omega program. I wanted to have no attachments when I listened to Pir Vilayat. Although my wife did not welcome the prospect of no family income, she saw that my search for knowledge and purpose in my life would not be fulfilled through my position as a bench technician. She knew my attraction to the Sufis, and supported me in my decision to investigate them with an unencumbered outlook. Her knowledge of my uncle's offer helped ease her mind.

I hoped that a miracle of sorts would happen while at Omega, and I would somehow get offered a position with Pir Vilayat's group, the Sufi Order of the West. They must have a need for an electronics technician, I reasoned. If that fell through, then I would be moving my family to my uncle's place in Silicon Valley.

## *September 1981, New Lebanon, NY*

"There's the Massachusetts state line. We missed it," I said as I stopped the car and waited for a chance to turn around.

We retraced our tracks back six-tenths of a mile to the turn-off, a small, easy-to-miss gravel road. I could see why the people in town who gave us directions told us the exact distance from the state line.

I turned onto the road. "Now only one mile to go."

"*Cha ta dah dee day, oh,*" our two-and-a-half-year-old son chortled from his car seat in the rear. He must have picked up our buoyant mood as we approached our destination.

The rough road kept our speed to a crawl and dragged out the final mile, ratcheting up our anticipation. Finally, we spied it, The Abode of the Message, a former Shaker Village that was home to approximately one hundred members of the Sufi Order of the West. We parked in the lot across the road and scrambled out to inspect the attractive campus.

Four large buildings enclosed a spacious quad full of grass and trees and two walkways, each cutting diagonally across the lawn and crossing in the middle. The weathered buildings gave the sense of a time long forgotten, the original, unadorned, hundred-year-old Shaker construction of unpainted wood siding being altered only by nature.

We walked along the paths to soak in the atmosphere and to stretch our legs, cramped from the long drive. The campus buzzed with activity on the bright, early fall day. A truck full of firewood pulled into one corner and men unloaded the fuel and stacked it in a three-sided shed along one of the buildings. Women stood talking to each other near the entrance to one building as they watched children playing with balls and sticks on the lawn. As we passed the open door of the building we saw other women working at sewing machines and carrying bolts of fabric and finished pieces of clothing.

After a leisurely tour around the compound we returned to the building with a sign stating "Visitor Information." Inside a thin man in his early thirties with short brown hair and wire-rimmed glasses introduced himself as Joseph. We explained our interest in learning how one might become a part of the community. As it was a few minutes past noon, he invited us to join him for lunch, which, he told us, was being served cafeteria style in the main dining area.

We helped ourselves to a vegetarian meal and joined our host at a table. Joseph was a quiet man. He exuded calmness, but was not withdrawn. He spoke only to answer our questions. When he talked he maintained a pleasant countenance and even eye contact. It seemed that he was gauging us, as if he wanted to peer into our souls and ascertain what we held in our depths. I understood his frame of mind. The growth and popularity of their community forced the Sufis to scrutinize potential initiates. Long periods of silence during the meal felt awkward at first, but I adjusted to their meditative quality and let myself enjoy them.

After the meal as we took another walk around the grounds, Aaron decided to run ahead of us to join a group of young boys playing together. These boys looked to be about two years older than our son. My wife seemed concerned about letting him go by himself, but the calmness we saw in Joseph influenced my response.

"Let him go. This place seems very peaceful," I said.

In less than a minute Aaron was crying and running to us after one of the boys wielded a stick like a sword and hit Aaron in the head. Meryl scooped up our child. Physically he was fine, but I knew that he suffered emotionally. With a brisker step than before, we walked to our car and left. This incident stripped some of the magic from the place for me, and, as my wife told me later, all of it for her. She couldn't abide the lack of parental control and oversight of the aggressive young boys that afternoon.

## *September 1981, Bennington, VT*

From the Sufi Village we headed to Bennington College in Bennington, VT. The Omega program, for which I had quit my job, took place on this beautiful, sprawling campus. Walking around the peaceful grounds full of abundant, leafy landscaping and meandering paths put us back in a spiritual mood, full of great anticipation. I knew Pir Vilayat's workshop would have a large audience. I arrived early to the venue and positioned myself in the middle of the auditorium, close to the front. I came by myself. My wife kept Aaron during this time, as I agreed to watch him later so she could attend a session of her choosing.

When Pir Vilayat walked onto the stage, he carried a conglomeration of what looked like Tinker Toy parts connected into a large, unusual shape. At the beginning of his talk he explained that the structure comprised a model of a crystal. He talked about the beauty of a crystal.

My attention riveted on him as he spoke about how the crystal could represent many things. The connection to my vision struck me as prophetic. I also remembered a passage in his book where he characterized the relationship between a teacher and student as a crystal.

What an auspicious beginning. I still had a vivid memory of the vision of the Sufis and the crystal they had stared into. Could this signify that I had a destiny with this man? I focused on him as he spoke. I attempted to block everything else out as my focus narrowed. The rest of the room became blurry until it completely disappeared from my awareness. Finally, I reached an altered state of awareness where I could see and hear only him.

Just as I achieved this condition he dropped his toy crystal and it shattered into pieces. The spell abruptly came to a halt. I remembered from his book that he had written that if either the teacher or student abused the trust in the relationship the crystal would break. I could not avoid the symbolism of what had happened. It felt as though our relationship had shattered before it had properly formed. The rest of the talk did not inspire me. It seemed vacuous and boring. I fought off a feeling of despair throughout the rest of the conference.

I returned home disheartened. A few weeks later I contacted my uncle to see if his offer still stood. He assured me that it did, but he thought I should wait until after Christmas. That way we wouldn't be missing our families during the holidays.

My wife didn't protest moving our family to the west coast. She knew it would upset her parents because they would miss their grandchildren, especially our two-month-old daughter, Adia, who arrived between the time of the Omega program and Christmas. Still, she supported my decision. She believed my uncle's pronouncement that with my experience I could make a good living in California. Plus her liberal beliefs and interest in New Age spirituality made California an attractive and exciting destination.

# Chapter 20

*April 1982, Palo Alto, CA*

I took the ear bud out and complained. "I don't want this in my ear. It's too distracting," I told the lady who had moments before instructed me to place the small plastic device in my ear. The thing had kept droning in a saccharine voice, "You are very relaxed. You feel very comfortable," and other mundane statements designed, I suppose, to ease any anxiety I might have about visiting a therapist whose specialties included hypnotism. But the words kept me from focusing on the question the therapist had just asked.

Without looking up at me, Ruth Este replied in a business-like fashion, "You have to keep it in. I can turn the volume down so it is subliminal, but you have to keep it in."

"Okay. Then please, do turn it down."

She put down her notepad and reached over to turn the volume knob on the cassette player. "A little more," I asked.

She turned the knob again. Finally, I could no longer hear anything. I smiled and said, "That's good."

She picked up her notepad. "Now tell me why you came to see me," she asked for a second time.

"Well, my aunt thought you might be able to help me out. I just moved out to California a couple of months ago, and I haven't been able to find a job," I told her as I twisted my body in my chair in order to look at her. The patient chair faced the wall with the therapist chair to the left looking on. In this contorted position I told her of my move to Silicon Valley and how it had left me less prosperous than I'd hoped. The recession of 1982 made job opportunities scarce, even for someone with a couple of years of experience as an electronics technician.

After three months of daily job searches, my aunt suggested that I see Ruth, because although she did have her therapist license, she also had a reputation as a clairvoyant.

As I explained my situation in detail she jotted down notes. When I finished she looked up at me with an intense stare and asked where I had applied. I told her of the numerous places where I left applications and the couple of places where I even had interviews and how I thought those interviews went.

She nodded, and then after I finished, she rattled off the names of several other electronic firms in the valley and cited different pros and cons with each one. For some she gave upbeat assessments, encouraging me to contact them. By this time I had grown tired of twisting in the chair to see my therapist, so I just looked straight forward. It probably looked like I didn't want to pay attention to what she had to say.

"Are you okay?" she asked.

"Oh, yes. Sure," I assured her. "I'm just tired of sitting that way," I said with a slight sideways glance.

"What are you feeling right now?" she asked. It seemed like she didn't trust my answer.

The question disarmed me and put me in a defensive mode. I reacted by simply clearing my mind, stopping my internal dialogue. "Nothing in particular," I told her. I forced myself to twist my head around again to look at my questioner and gave her a soft smile while I persisted in stopping my inner dialogue. I really didn't have a concern and I just wanted to remain as open minded as possible, so I tried to show that.

After a moment's pause her eyes opened wider. "Who are you?" she asked abruptly.

"What do you mean? You know who I am. I already told you," I said, feeling confused.

"Why did you take Brian's body?"

"What are you talking about? Nobody took my body."

"I bet you don't know anything about Brian's childhood." She put down the notepad and glared at me. "Who was your best friend when you were young?"

It took me a moment to register that she spoke to me as if talking to another being, and that the question about my childhood was an apparent effort to show that some entity had taken possession of my body.

My confusion made it difficult to register her question and form a response. Finally, I stammered an answer. "Tom. Tom Moore." A wave of sadness hit me as I recalled my old friend. "He was killed in an auto accident."

"See!" My answer seemed to provide confirmation to Ruth that she spoke to someone other than Brian.

I stared at her without a clue about how to respond.

"You are very, very old. You are from another time. Your shirt has ruffled sleeves. What do you want?"

The features of Ruth's face went out of focus as she spoke. Then, instead of the woman, I saw a clown in garish makeup.

She continued, "Now you are a young woman with a high collar. You are very beautiful."

Ruth's face morphed into a caricature of a squirrel with long whiskers and large front teeth. What she said made no sense, but my mind didn't dwell on her comments. Instead I pondered her changed facial appearance. It seemed as though she was either clowning around, or she had lost it, gone completely squirrely on me.

After a few moments of silence she spoke again, but in a subdued voice.

"I believe you are going to become a medium in the very near future," she told me in a serious voice.

It took a while to first register that she again addressed me directly and then to realize what she meant. I didn't hesitate in my response. "I'm not interested in becoming a medium," I told her in a cold tone. I had read popular books concerning mediums and how some people would go into a trance and another personality would take over. Purportedly the personality lived in another time and place and the person's soul traveled in some mysterious, unknown fashion to temporarily take over the host's body.

What I could see for me in that path involved not fame or adulation, but rather scorn and ridicule. I could see people calling me crazy for thinking I could host another person's spirit. I couldn't see the half-full glass of those finding it interesting or praiseworthy.

"That doesn't matter," she said. "You just wait and see."

I thought that channeling the spirit of another being could provide nothing but trouble for me. Besides, what was she seeing and thinking? I hadn't felt anything unusual. My conscious self did not experience any change. I wanted to put the episode behind me. I left the session with Ruth Este without any insight for my job search and feeling confused about what she had said.

In the evening after my visit with Ruth I took a short walk from my uncle's house in Menlo Park to a bookstore with a large section of titles on philosophies and Eastern thought. I saw a section on Gurdjieff that contained the Ouspensky tomes that captivated me three years earlier. A book by Fritz Peters in this section drew me in. Peters spent many of his formative years at Gurdjieff's country manor in France, where Gurdjieff taught. He wrote about his experiences there in *Boyhood with Gurdjieff*.

I opened the book to a one-page biography on Gurdjieff, located in the introduction, and noticed the date of Gurdjieff's death. After a quick calculation in my head it hit me like a cement truck. My birthday came nine months and two days after the day he died—the normal gestation period for a human. I knew that when Buddhists look for the reincarnation of their spiritual leader, the Dali Lama, they look for a child born nine months after the death of the previous leader.

My mind searched for an explanation of the time between Gurdjieff's death and my birth. The scientist part of me wanted to argue in favor of coincidence, but another part of me did not let it argue. That part of my mind just acknowledged the fact and tried to turn off the inner dialogue. I did not need to debate reincarnation versus coincidence with myself. What possible good would that accomplish?

I walked back to the house trying to stop my inner dialogue, but a flood of memories from *In Search of the Miraculous* about Gurdjieff's escape from Russia during the revolution wouldn't let go of me. I remembered how I would go into a trance after reading only a page or two of the book. A large, rational part of me wanted to ignore all this, wanted to deny any connection between Gurdjieff's existence and mine, but another part took control and pursued the idea and looked for an alternative rational explanation.

My mind went back to Ouspensky's book, *The Fourth Way*, where he wrote about the Law of Seven. The octave in music theory represents the most common example of this law. Of course the octave consists of eight notes but two are 'do'. Do, re, mi, fa, so, la, and ti comprise the seven unique notes. This law manifested itself in each person in the seven chakras. In the universe at large the Law of Seven produces something Gurdjieff called the Ray of Creation, from which followed the old adage "as above, so below."

The top step in the Ray of Creation, the 'do' if you use the octave metaphor, refers to the Absolute, the all-encompassing. Gurdjieff called the next step, the 'ti', of the musical octave analogy, 'All Worlds', followed by 'All Suns' as 'la', and then our own sun as 'so'. All of the planets of our solar system rest in the 'fa' position. The planet Earth forms the next step, the role of 'mi' in creation's scale, and the moon has the role of 're'. The last step, the final 'do' in the Ray of Creation, Gurdjieff again calls the Absolute, this time referring to the void, or absence of everything.

I thought about how we all have a gravitational connection with each of the seven slots in the Ray of Creation. The Earth's gravitational pull we feel much more than any other, but we see the effect of the pull of the moon in the changing of the tides, and although not everyone notices the effect of the phases of the moon on their mood, many do. The sun does, without doubt, exert a gravitational pull on us as individuals. However, we cannot directly measure the extent of that pull. We can say the same thing about the gravity of the galaxy that we spin in. These various gravitational fields are distinct. Do they create distinct entities within us?

Swami Rama's discussion about the different bodies came to me and generated an idea. Does each body owe its existence to a connection with a particular gravitational field? It seemed a simple, yet elegant way to identify a mechanism responsible for the astral body and the mental body.

What if we can separate the self into different bodies based on gravitational field? Maybe only the physical body dies upon death and the higher bodies survive. Some books on yoga mention astral travel and discuss techniques that can give a person the ability to leave the physical body and travel in the astral body. The astral body usually gets characterized as a light, ethereal form, a body of light and energy, only with no solid mass. Can a person learn how to differentiate the gravitational effects of the moon or sun from that of the earth within him or herself and then travel in that body influenced only by a gravitational field different than the Earth's?

Likewise, upon death of the physical body, perhaps the mental body of the person, or the portion of the person under the influence of the gravitational pull of the sun or even perhaps the Milky Way galaxy, leaves the physical body and enters another newly created human physical body. A possible explanation for reincarnation!

While thinking about my possible past incarnation, another thought grabbed me. What about Greg, whom I'd insulted and performed pseudo-esoteric dances for at SKY Land? From our conversations I knew he was almost two full years older than me. I checked my Ouspensky book and found that Ouspensky died just shy of two years before Gurdjieff.

Ouspensky was Gurdjieff's most famous student. Ouspensky's books spread the notoriety and teachings of Gurdjieff more than any other vehicle. The two collaborated on esoteric dancing before an acrimonious split. People who believe in reincarnation often claim that when you are reborn you often seek out people with whom you have an incomplete relationship. Did "Karma," as I told Greg, best explain my bizarre dancing behavior of that June day?

So with these thoughts—the discovery that Gurdjieff died nine months before I was born and Greg's birth after Ouspensky's death—part of me reached the conviction that the death of Gurdjieff led to my birth, or rather the death of Gurdjieff's body allowed the mind that had occupied his body to enter my newly conceived body.

However, another part of me stayed skeptical. As a student I learned well the conventional doctrine that reincarnation could not happen. Humans evolved from natural selection. Period. End of story. I could not see a path for natural selection of the astral body or for a mental body that could reincarnate.

With this internal debate about reincarnation coursing through my thoughts I could not sleep. Around 1:30 in the morning I tried to relax by using breathing techniques I learned in yoga classes. I watched my respiration as it got slower and slower. After following my breathing in and out for a few minutes, on one long exhale I felt my consciousness leave my body along with my breath. I had total awareness of thought processes but no awareness of a body.

I didn't experience a feeling of astral travel. There was no recognizable form of light that corresponded to my physical body. Rather, I had exited my physical body to exist in a formless manner into a world with no light. I had no awareness of my body or anything other than my thoughts. It seemed that I existed only in mental form, or as yoga philosophy would say in my mental body, although I had no sense of a body.

I found this undetermined time away from the body relaxing. When my physical body finally gasped an inhalation and my awareness returned to normal, I had more energy than ever. Not until almost 4:00 in the morning did I finally fall asleep.

## CHAPTER 21

*April 1982, Palo Alto, CA*

Despite not having much sleep that night, I felt refreshed the following morning, a Saturday. With the edge of the high from the previous day worn off, I felt less hyper and somewhat mellowed. I still felt a bit of the excitement, though, and had no hunger. I did try to eat something, thinking I would have a horrible crash if I didn't, but food had no appeal. I couldn't force myself to eat.

Sometime after noon I wandered into the side yard, an area with several pine trees. Upon arrival there I froze as a golden eagle flew through the pines and perched on the ground less than ten yards from where I stood. Not a real golden eagle, though, but an apparition of one.

This sighting differed from my vision of the crystal. In my vision of the three Sufis I first closed my eyes. At this time the apparition appeared among the natural landscape, and although I knew that no physical bird sat in front of me, I did not question the existence of the image on some level. I had heard claims of objects manifesting themselves from the astral world. This seemed to fit that description. Was this eagle from the world under gravitational influence primarily associated with the sun?

Mainstream psychology would classify my experience as a hallucination created only in my mind, but to me that explanation didn't fit. My mind at the time had no disturbing thoughts. I felt collected and calm enjoying the mild, sunny California day. I was not having a sleep-deprived hallucination, either, since I had slept for a couple of hours, at least. What I saw I took as a message or sign from an astral being.

I put out my hand to show friendship to the bird. As soon as I made this gesture the bird dissolved into a shimmering light, and I watched as it beamed into the palm of my hand in a matter of two or three seconds. When the transfer of this radiant force completed, I instinctively put my hand over my navel and felt a surge encapsulate my solar plexus.

I held my hand there several seconds while the warmth of the energy gave me a feeling of well-being. After about fifteen seconds the wave of heat subsided and I relaxed the muscles in my arm in anticipation of dropping the arm to my side, however, even though my muscles relaxed my arm remained in position, as if glued to the spot. I smiled. It seemed as though the energy from the eagle hadn't all been absorbed yet. I waited another thirty seconds before again trying to move my hand away from my navel, and this time succeeded.

This encounter with the phantasmal eagle gave my mental landscape another twist. Now it seemed that a being had contacted me from a different level, the astral plane. Did someone want to communicate through me, like Ruth had suggested? Or did some entity just want to contact me in some less intrusive way? I still had an aversion to the idea of hosting another being. I wanted to keep control of my body and not let it be used by another spirit. However, I did want to explore the second idea, communication only, but without opening myself up to a label of mental instability or craziness.

I walked around to the back of the house, still feeling the effects of the energy absorbed from the dissolved eagle. I sat down at the picnic table in the shade of a ponderosa pine tree and contemplated the significance of what just happened. I felt the dichotomy of wanting to try to communicate on this new level and wanting to dismiss the idea as nonsense. It didn't take long to decide. I couldn't ignore what had happened. The appearance of the bird felt like a magical gift that once opened had to be seen through to the end. As I sat listening to birds in the pleasant California day I resolved to open my mind instead of closing it.

Communicating on a different plane presents the problem of knowing what to believe. The mind can make up things so easily that we can fool ourselves without knowing it. I didn't want to believe or not to believe that some being wanted to communicate with me on another level of existence. I wanted to remain neutral, so I practiced clearing my mind. I made an effort to "stop my inner dialogue" using familiar meditation techniques and focusing only on my surroundings.

Those who speak of visits to the astral or causal world talk about the propensity for a person's beliefs to dictate the directions and encounters they have on those levels of existence. Without a doubt,

Carlos Castaneda's writing had a serious impact on my mental development. Through his books I spent several years in my early twenties under the influence of his ideas. However, after finding the teachings of Gurdjieff, I no longer felt drawn to what Castaneda had to say. Gurdjieff seemed to explain things better, and, in effect, these ideas replaced those that Castaneda had planted in me. In fact, I never purchased the most recent book by Castaneda. I had read all of his earlier works, but when his fifth book, *The Eagle's Gift*, came out earlier that year, I no longer felt drawn to his ideas and as a result had not bought it or read it. At times I thought about buying it, but I never followed though.

As I sat in the shade trying to clear my mind, it struck me what the appearance of the shimmering golden eagle meant. It appeared as a gift in the form of the enormous positive energy I gained. I gave myself a chuckle with the thought that I had finally discovered the story of the eagle's gift. My mind leaped to a hypothetical question: Did the phantasmagorical eagle represent my connection on the astral plane to Castaneda?

When this question first came to me I sensed a presence in the mental, or as some call it, the causal world. I don't know how to explain this feeling other than to say it seemed as if I could feel the existence of another being. This recognition didn't occur through a conversation because it happened without words. It seemed more like we took measure of each other in our minds' eyes. I recognized this entity as the mind of Carlos Castaneda. The familiar voice of Castaneda's writings came through, not in an audible manner, but through recognition of his thoughts.

When this occurred, part of me felt stupid for thinking I had really contacted Castaneda in this way, but another part of me felt that we actually sensed each other on a different level of existence. This part surmised that my focus at that time centered not on my physical body or astral body, but rather on my mental form. Esoteric schools claim that both the astral and causal (mental) bodies reside within the physical body. When one travels in the astral body, the mental body goes along. When one's mental body separates, it goes alone.

The mental body separated from my physical and astral bodies the night before. By limiting my food intake, did I keep this focus intact? It seemed that I could and did move on the mental plane to where I could connect with the mind of Castaneda. I sat under the tree oblivious to my surroundings, lost in a thought exchange.

# Chapter 22

*April 1982, Menlo Park area, CA*

It didn't take more than a few moments, maybe a minute or two, of what seemed like a telepathic encounter with Castaneda before I broke from my reverie and stood up. It felt too strange to continue. I sensed that I needed to escape my mental realm and connect back to the "real world." As I walked around to the back of the house I spied my uncle's bike inside the open garage door. I had his permission to ride it whenever I wanted. It seemed like the perfect way to engage in something physical. I maneuvered past a garden rake and my aunt's cultivator and took the ten-speed off its hook on the wall. After connecting the foot pump and getting the pressure up to fifty-five pounds I wheeled it out of the garage.

When I reached the side porch, I called in to Meryl, who was in the dining room feeding lunch to the children.

"Honey, I'm going on a bike ride."

"Don't you want to eat some lunch first?" she asked.

"No. I'm not hungry now." The thought of food still did not appeal to me.

"Are you sure?"

"Yes. I'll be back before too long."

I took off down Middle Avenue, heading toward my favorite biking destination, Atherton. Its secluded streets with lush landscaping hid the expensive homes and I could pretend that I rode on rural roads. I pedaled along at a comfortable pace trying to forget about the golden eagle and the weird mental exchange with Castaneda. My mind soon cleared from the internal chatter that accompanied all the preparations for the ride as I got into a rhythm. When I did this, Castaneda's presence returned.

It seemed like he wanted to know my identity, but I didn't hear a voice saying, "Who are you?" Instead I simply felt as if someone wanted me to reveal myself on the mental plane of existence.

When ignoring the persistent inquiry didn't work, I tried to project my personal character to the intruding mind. I didn't attempt to use words to convey the idea, but rather by thinking how I would feel in front of him with my chest pushed out. I stood up from the bike seat and pedaled in a defiant way, but after concentrating on the mental pose for a minute in this fashion I tired of the position. When I relaxed back down into the saddle I sensed another thought wave from what I perceived as Castaneda's consciousness. That entity seemed to somehow recognize me as Gurdjieff.

This confused me. Castaneda must know that Gurdjieff died over thirty years ago. Did he want to make contact with a dead person? Maybe he wanted to channel Gurdjieff. That didn't sound like Castaneda. Did some other person want to channel Gurdjieff? Maybe Castaneda, or whoever it was, recognized me as the reincarnation of Gurdjieff. These thoughts jumbled together as I rode.

I came to a stop sign on Atherton Avenue where I hooked a right and headed for El Camino Royal. I didn't usually bike in that much traffic, but something had pulled me in that direction, and as usual I followed my instincts. *Maybe I don't need the secluded streets today. Maybe if I hit the main drag it will provide some needed distractions*, I rationalized. As the traffic picked up, I couldn't help wondering whether the interruptions of what seemed like another mind resembled what schizophrenics experienced. *Am I going crazy?*

After a couple blocks of cruising along the busy thoroughfare I realized that my hope of escaping the thought interchange through engaging more traffic had proved futile. It seemed like the other mind kept repeating the desire to know about Gurdjieff. With all the moving vehicles to focus on I didn't have enough mental resources to form any coherent mental response to the recurring interruptions and I couldn't find a way to ignore them. Questions began to swirl in my head. *Am I Gurdjieff? Should I think of myself as Gurdjieff? Should I go back to being Gurdjieff? How could I go back to being Gurdjieff?*

I don't know if the intensity of the traffic or the annoying questions prompted me to turn, or maybe some non-volitional force took over, but I turned off El Camino Royal onto a side street. I needed to quit fighting traffic.

As I pedaled away from the busy traffic the Gurdjieff questions persisted. I tried to block them out, but Castaneda's presence returned. Castaneda had exercised enormous influence over the development of thought in my life. I wondered if by going back to the mind of Gurdjieff I could free myself from Castaneda's influence in the mental plane, where I found myself struggling with him. Going back to my life as Gurdjieff would make sense if it applied only to my mental makeup. It would mean wiping out the influence of those who had molded me during this incarnation.

For a second I found this twist of logic encouraging before coming back to reality and muttering, "But that's impossible."

Yet as I heard myself say that, another bizarre thought popped into my mind. Why not try some reverse psychology? Rather than trying to ignore the barrage of Gurdjieff questions, why not play devil's advocate and mess with the source of the questions? I mused about how I would get back to the intellectual existence of Gurdjieff.

I'd read enough sci-fi and seen enough *Star Trek* episodes in my youth to have some bizarre thoughts on the topic fill my mind. Maybe I would go back in time to live as Gurdjieff to change something that would alter the timeline in the space-time continuum. Or maybe there was an alternate universe where I could escape, leaving my physical body behind. I let these thoughts permeate my mind. It gave me a smile to see humor in the crazy ideas and not take the thought interchange too seriously.

This reverie lasted until I came to a complex of buildings I didn't recognize. *Is this some sort of campus?* I wondered. I jumped off my bike and headed toward a large building that sat behind an expansive parking lot, thinking that I might find a water fountain inside.

# CHAPTER 23

*April 1982, Redwood City, CA*

"Go back! Go back!"

The words came from a lone figure standing near the far corner of the parking lot. I stared at the man. He appeared to be in his late twenties, dressed in jeans and t-shirt, and wearing dark glasses.

After several seconds his voice rang out again. "No! No! Go back! Go back!"

*This guy can't be yelling at me*, I told myself as I walked across the lot, keeping as far away from the voice as possible. "I'm not going back to being Gurdjieff," I said under my breath as I looked around hoping to see the target of the cry. No one. Only a sea of cars with chrome glistening in the sunlight.

"This is crazy," I mumbled.

The mental world had just spilled over into the real world. A sense of panic filled me.

I spied a small area next to the entrance of one of the buildings where I could stash my bike. I headed for it.

"No! No! Go back! Go back!"

*What's going on?* I wondered. *There's nothing around him. Who's he yelling at?* Although somehow I felt I knew the answer.

I walked toward the doors of the building which had taken on an inviting, shimmering look. *Like a magic palace*, I thought, *a refuge.*

A group of five men in their late twenties or early thirties exited just before I reached the door. They struck me as unusually quiet and sober for a bunch of young guys hanging out together. As they passed they glared at me, trying to look tough.

Just before I opened the door I heard the voice from around the corner again. "Go back! Go back!"

Inside the building the quiet felt like a warm security blanket. I gave a sigh of relief as I walked down a long corridor. Before I could contemplate where to go to relax, my autopilot took over. It seemed like my body knew what direction to take. I turned to see a door that had a glow similar to what the entrance had exhibited a moment ago. I twisted the doorknob, not knowing what to expect. I had the surreal feeling of unlocking a doorway to an enchanted room.

The door opened. The thought of a water fountain no longer registered on my consciousness as I entered the room in a near mystical trance.

The room appeared to be some kind of lounge or waiting area; chairs lined the walls to my right and left with several small stands filled with magazines and newspapers dispersed between them. Two men occupied the room. An obese young man with long, dark, unkempt hair and dressed in a tie-dyed t-shirt sat on the left near the entrance reading a newspaper, and a rather short, middle-aged Hispanic man sat in the third chair to my right staring straight ahead.

At the far end of the room two high windows let in natural light that gave the room a strange haunting glow, even with the overhead fluorescent lights all on. Beneath each of the windows sat a comfortable-looking seat. I walked toward them, pulling a magazine from one of the stands as I crossed the room.

When I reached the chair situated beneath the left window I gazed outside. The sky somehow looked alive with lines of energy streaking down, providing that magical glow I'd felt when I first stepped into the room. I remembered seeing something like these years earlier. I had connected them with Castaneda's "lines of the world" back then. It brought me back to the Castaneda-Gurdjieff mental struggle that I wanted to forget and twisted my short-lived enchantment into bewitchment. I made a grimace as I sat down in the chair. I wanted to wait out this craziness I felt. I wanted my normalcy back.

"Go back! No! No! Go back!"

I could hear his voice through the window.

I did not have time to brood before the five men I'd passed just a minute before barged into the room. Their tough looks intensified my already uneasy feeling.

The Hispanic man rose and gestured to the chairs on either side of him. They seated themselves and remained silent. The older man sat back down and looked straight ahead. I looked at them for only a moment and then, not wanting to feel self-conscious, I opened my magazine and put it in front of my face.

"Paranoia takes two to tango," I remembered from the Ram Dass tape. *If I don't feel fear, nothing can happen,* I told myself. *We are in a public building and I am safe from them. They can't do anything to me.* Why a public building would have immunity from violence never crossed my mind, but I needed something to reassure me and logic seemed to be breaking down, so I took to wishful thinking.

"Go back! Now! Go back!" His plea contained an intense emotion, even in its muffled form.

*He sounds like a crow*, I thought. *A raven controlled by some dark force.* The thought distressed me. I wanted to see things in a more positive vein, so I tried to block out the voice.

I glanced out the window again. Everything still seemed as though it throbbed with the energy of faint glowing light trails. *What am I seeing? ...Maybe meditation will help.* I slipped my shoes off, pulled my legs up and sat cross-legged on the soft seat while keeping the magazine in front of my face. I tried to rid my mind of the distracting thoughts by closing my eyes and focusing on my breath.

"Go back!" The cry returned. "You must go back!"

*I am back*, I told myself. *This is back. This is forward. This is everything.* As I tried to block out the voice an image of a large flame engulfed me. The image reminded me of protesting Buddhist monks who doused themselves with gasoline and set themselves on fire to protest the war in Vietnam. I knew that I wasn't on fire, but I felt like a protestor. I didn't want this situation to continue, so I let myself "burn." It created anguish within me, but I felt powerless to do anything about it.

"Anyone got a match?" A voice from one of the men broke the silence.

The flame image disappeared. I opened my eyes a slit and peered over my magazine. The comment sounded like it came from the blond man sitting closest to me with a smirk on his face. He had no cigarette to be lit. Moreover, by his intonation I sensed that he referred to my self-image and not to a cigarette.

Sheer terror gripped me. My pulse raced along with my thoughts. *Am I hearing things? If I'm hearing things I need to just relax. On the other hand, if he really said what I thought he said, then I must pretend that I didn't hear him.* Paranoia takes two.

I repeated this argument over several times in slightly different versions. For a brief moment I thought about leaving, but I didn't want to show fear. No paranoia. Finally, I managed to bring my heart rate under control. As I gained a bit of self-confidence I closed my eyes to meditate again. The flame image reappeared.

As I focused on the image of fire, I heard a voice beside me. "That looks like a firebird." I opened my eyes and glanced to my right. The Hispanic man stood there looking out the window. He'd spoken in a casual tone and with an inflection that expected a confirmation from someone.

It generated an automatic reaction in me, like he had momentarily had some kind of power over me. I felt compelled to check out what he saw, but as I uncrossed my legs and placed my feet on the floor I realized the absurdity of the remark. Instead of standing up and walking over to the window, I crouched down beside the chair and fumbled with my shoes, half in fear and half in bewilderment.

*"When improper thoughts arise, ponder the opposite."* The passage from the Yoga Sutras flashed into my mind.

*Ponder the opposite,* I repeated to myself. As I said this I felt the flame engulf me again.

*What is the opposite?* I wondered, feeling a panicky rush to find an answer to this hypothetical question.

It came in a flash. The opposite of a firebird is a penguin.

Immediately I thought: *I'm freezing. I'm in the middle of the Antarctic and it's fifty degrees below zero. I'm hanging out with a bunch of penguins. I am a penguin keeping an egg warm under my toes.* It seemed to work. At least I no longer felt as though a flame surrounded me.

The man left the window and returned to his chair. My fear subsided and I began to feel self-conscious about my unusual squatting position. I stood and peered out the window.

"Yes, that's a firebird all right," I remarked trying to sound matter-of-fact. "That's funny, I was just thinking about penguins when you said that."

A lie, since I hadn't thought about the penguins until after he had mentioned the firebird, but I felt the need to appear one step ahead of him. This smooth line contrasted with my racing, disjointed thoughts. *Either that was the most bizarre set of coincidences I ever heard, or these folks possessed abnormal perceptions. A match? A firebird? They must know of my struggle with the flame image. And if they do, why would they torment me like this?*

I sat back down cross-legged on the chair. *They don't seem hostile, though*, I reassured myself as I glanced around the room. The men did not have unfriendly looks anymore. They simply looked bored. *Maybe it's just my imagination or my nerves.*

"Go back! You must go back!" the voice intoned again.

By now I almost anticipated it, and although I couldn't say it gave me comfort to hear it, I could deal with it without increasing my anxiety. *I am back. I was back. I will be back. There is nowhere else to go*, I droned to myself, like a mantra, in response to the voice.

On an impulse I got up from the chair and slipped my shoes back on my feet. I couldn't just sit there anymore, and the thought of leaving felt cowardly and fear-induced. I wouldn't allow that feeling to take over. I walked a few steps toward the men.

I had no idea what to say so I just spoke the truth. "I'm kind of nervous," I said to the group in the most composed way I could muster. I felt like a politician addressing a skeptical crowd.

After a couple seconds I continued, "I'm waiting for my wife." A lie, but the truth had sounded so lame. The lie made it sound like someone might be joining me soon. I saw it as a hedge on my bout with fear.

In an instant came a sarcastic reply from the Hispanic. "What's she going to bring? A little bit of God?"

The caustic tone of his voice caught me off guard, but I didn't let it show. I considered to myself, *God is good, and if she did come, she would bring good.* I answered without hesitation, "Yes, sure," with a broad grin.

"What are you going to do then? Walk on water?" the man returned another sarcastic barb.

I remembered the feeling of floating away the previous night. "Yeah, maybe even air," I responded in a gleeful tone to disguise my anxiety about the absurd conversation.

The man stared at me for a moment before speaking in an authoritative, urgent manner. "He needs something." He paused then added, "Go get him some water." He gestured to the door.

The five left the room. The Hispanic man followed them to the door, but stopped in the doorway looking in the direction where the men disappeared.

At that instant, I realized the identity of this person. The one with whom I communicated on the mental plane over the past hour, Carlos

Castaneda, stood in front of me. I put the pieces together. He fit the physical description of Castaneda, a short, stocky Hispanic. The other men deferred to him. This guy held the alpha position. The famous sorcerer had a well-known entourage, of sorts, that followed him... his protégés. Dudes and chicks who wanted to emulate him. The guy chanting outside had to be part of his posse, too.

In Castaneda's books he wrote about how he followed "lines of force" in his quests, the lines of force that appeared stronger than ever moments ago out the window. His work also explained how he had perceptions of energy lines emanating from people. That explained the comments that he and the one other in the group made about a match and firebird. They must have seen a change in my energy field or aura that indicated flames.

Why would he first hurl sarcastic comments to a perfect stranger and then right away want to help me? In his story about meeting his teacher, Don Juan, Carlos described how Don Juan did not pick him, but that the universe led his teacher to him. It seemed like Castaneda's presence linked directly to mine. He came there to meet and interact with me.

The vision of the eagle, the telepathic thoughts, the lines of force, the voice outside the window, and the ability to see my personal turmoil, all of this made sense to me now. My karma with Castaneda had led me to this encounter. I felt unmistakable recognition. What agenda did he have? Why did he want to help me? What did he expect from me, a pledge of loyalty?

I stood still for several long seconds piecing together everything. Then I spoke to him.

"I really enjoyed the eagle's gift."

My vision of the golden eagle had started this whole episode of astral and causal experiences. It had given me the energy that eventually led to this encounter, so I told the truth, but I also told Castaneda a lie. I had never read his book *The Eagle's Gift*. Somehow speaking this double entendre gave me a secret pleasure and a confidence boost.

When I mentioned the eagle's gift, the man at the door looked back at me. We locked eyes for several seconds then he appeared to nod with a quick jerk in the direction taken by the other men. Then he took off after the others without saying anything. *Was he signaling me to follow him?*

I felt a surge of relief accompanied by an intense curiosity—relief because I no longer sensed a struggle on the mental plane, and curiosity because I wanted to understand the agenda of this troupe of men I had encountered under such strange circumstances. After a moment of indecision I took hurried steps out of the room.

I walked down the hall in the direction the man had gone, but after passing through a door into another corridor I lost sight of him. I felt disappointment at missing an opportunity to communicate with someone I had once almost revered. Walking down the new hallway I noticed an open door on the right and ducked in hoping to find the men there.

I found myself in a much smaller room with only a few chairs and a single occupant, an older man with a dark beard. I entered, and with a feeling of disappointment, closed the door and sat down to ponder what had just happened. After a moment or two of replaying the past few minutes a feeling of discomfort crept into my awareness. The only other person in the room kept looking up from his notebook at me, making me feel self-conscious in the strange place, so I left.

I backtracked down the corridor, and when I reached the room I had first entered, I peered in and saw the man I had identified as Castaneda, along with his group of followers. Without a second thought I re-entered the room, excited by the opportunity to continue our interaction. As I walked toward the seat I had only minutes ago occupied I felt a strange sensation around my waist. It felt like energy leaving from my navel. A second surge of energy exited in quick succession.

"Oh, no!" came a cry from the blond. "Two of them."

With this comment I remembered something Castaneda wrote about the lines of force of the physical body. He claimed we each have a large bundle of energy concentrated in the navel area, and if someone had children, a hole in the energy appeared in the navel bundle for each child. A trained person could see these lines of force and detect the holes left by children. I had two children. I felt certain that this man referred to seeing those holes.

According to Don Juan, Castaneda's teacher, in order to walk the earth as a true warrior one had to close the holes in his or her energy field, a major undertaking for a student seeking this path to knowledge and power. According to Don Juan, this meant that one had to let go of the feeling that one's child depended on you.

The remark, and especially the tone of the remark, indicated to me that these people anticipated working with me in some way. Not because they chose me, but because the lines of the world led them to me. The exact purpose of their encounter with me, though, remained cloudy, but the thought of associating with someone with two children must not have appealed to one of them.

After I sat down I noticed a small tray with some food and a glass of water on the stand beside my seat.

I stared at Castaneda and his posse, but none of them looked back. They all had serious, distant looks. The men and the reason for our meeting grabbed all of my attention. Did I want to join them, as it seemed they expected to happen? I took off my wedding ring. Based on my understanding of the teachings of Castaneda it seemed apparent that I had to choose between this group and my family.

I plunked the ring down on the stand with a loud noise, as though I had called a meeting to order. I looked again at the men. Still none of them looked toward me. They all stared straight ahead, in effect saying, *"Your move."*

I thought about my one-time desire to leave Pennsylvania and search the southwest for Castaneda. Then I thought about my wife and family and how I had not lived up to expectations as a father and provider since quitting my job over six months ago. The place in my heart that held the love I felt toward my wife and children made me weak by this group's standards, but I couldn't let it go.

While my thoughts sifted through my dilemma, I took a long drink from the water on the stand next to me. Then, without thinking, I picked up the spoon from the tray and took a bite of what looked like some kind of pudding.

"*Pppppppt*," I spit the goop back out. Whether I just didn't like its artificial flavor or I came to my senses about eating something that I had no idea of its origin, I don't know. It didn't matter. Something said not to eat it.

In an instant came a short staccato, "*Tih*," from the leader of the group.

The sound seemed to convey an idea, like an affirmation. Like he agreed that I shouldn't eat the stuff. I thought about that interpretation for a second, and then reconsidered. Maybe he didn't mean anything. I wanted to ask him about it, but his distant stare kept my mind from forming the question.

While I contemplated what to say or do, an emotion formed within me. It seemed to bubble up, and then to my surprise I vocalized a *"Dh,"* which, after I said it, seemed to confirm his comment. Like saying, "Of course, I see what you mean."

The man sat looking straight ahead. After a long pause, his voice broke the silence with a *"Bh."*

I looked at him for a visual cue. I could see none. *What does "Bh" mean?* I asked myself. It sounded expectant, like something's about to happen, to bust out. I thought a bit and then nodded my head. I agreed. I hoped something would soon happen. I wanted to get everything out in the open. I let out a short *"Tih,"* hoping to convey my agreement.

I waited through another tense pause. Then with a *"Nnn,"* the short man continued the confusing conversation.

This reply caused me to wince. It seemed negative and controlling, and I couldn't fathom why. It conflicted with the idea I had a moment ago about him wanting to get things going. Without thinking I let out a frustrated, loud *"Kh."*

There was only a short pause before a reply of *"Dh."*

To me, this sound indicated he expected my frustration and could care less about it. It made my temper simmer. I let out a low growling *"Rrr"* sound, venting this irritation.

An instant *"Pppt"* came as a response, an almost mechanical rejection of my growl from the group leader, as if to say, *"Don't get aggressive with me. I'll chew you up and spit you out."*

I'd had enough. "Bullshit!" I spoke out loud in an angry voice. I could see the folly of entertaining the idea of joining his entourage. The interchange of weird expressions reminded me of my own personal dream of understanding the emotions behind sounds that led to my vision of the Sufis and the pointing to the Tufts graduate program. I knew from that limited interchange that my dreams would not happen with that group. I needed to establish my own mental space and free myself of Castaneda's influence for good, not get under it again.

I picked up my ring and put it back on, entering the decision of "no" to the question of joining their group. The men remained silent and staring straight ahead.

At this point I felt a stubborn streak arise within me. *I can play your game, too,* I said to myself. I stared straight ahead without registering the presence of the men for what seemed like an eternity. *I don't need them*, I kept telling myself.

After a long period of silence the leader finally spoke. "This place is a lair." He sprang up from his seat in a nimble, cat-like movement and left the room with his troupe traipsing along behind.

# Chapter 24

*April 1982, Menlo Park, CA*

When I got home I didn't tell my wife about all of the strange things that happened. I wanted the event over and forgotten about. After eating a big meal I spent the remainder of the day playing with my children and feeling happy that I'd chosen my family over a chance to hang out with a one-time hero.

The struggle on the mental plane returned a few times in the next two or three days whenever I thought about the event, but I could keep from getting entwined again by interacting with my family members. Each time the intruding thoughts took less and less effort to ignore. By the middle of the week I could think about the episode without any mental disturbance.

Toward the end of the week, my wife took the children for a walk to the park. I stayed at home working on my uncle's KayPro II personal computer. After an intense hour I took a break and sat down on a rug to meditate.

After a short while I entered a deep meditative state, and after one very smooth and long exhalation I felt my breathing stop. This led to an uncontrolled sensation of floating, and then all of a sudden I found my astral self sitting on a bench located on the top of a little knoll in a spacious park. I looked around trying to identify the location, but it didn't seem familiar. I surveyed the areas where I saw children playing in the distance, hoping to see my family, but I didn't see them anywhere.

Then my gaze fell on some people I did recognize—the man I knew as Castaneda and three of his men I had encountered a week before. They sat fifty to sixty yards away on top of a stone wall that bordered a path that weaved down a gentle slope. In an instinctive reaction I hunched down to avoid detection. Too late. One of them spied me and pointed in my direction.

Before I could decide what to do, they started toward me. They didn't follow the curvature of the path, but instead floated straight toward me in a single file. It took them less than two seconds to reach me. I put my arms above my head as they passed over, but I kept an eye on them. None of them did anything as they passed by, except the last, the ringleader. As he buzzed over I felt a shock or burn as he touched my forearm.

The pain from the leader's contact caused me to take a deep breath and I found myself back on my uncle's rug. I thought I'd finished with that group, and now this. I called Ruth Este's office and made an appointment. Ruth seemed like the best person for advice on dealing with the strange events of the past week. I couldn't confide in my wife. She would only get scared or think I'd lost my mind.

"What's happened with you since I saw you last time?" Ruth asked as soon as she finished adjusting the volume in the device in my ear.

When I finished describing the details of my first encounter with the strange entourage, Ruth said, "They call that a psychic attack. Do you know who they were?"

"Yes, I think so. I believe it was Carlos Castaneda and some of his followers."

She knit her brows. "He's a very powerful guy."

I nodded. "Do you know anything about astral travel?" I asked her.

"Yes, I sure do."

"Well, I saw these same people while in my astral body a few days later."

"Did they do anything to hurt you?"

"No. Uh, well, I did get pinched or something when in astral form, but nothing happened to my physical body."

Her eyes were wider than usual as she kept them fixed on me. "My astral body has been attacked and scratched so that it has left scars on my physical arms."

From her solemn look I knew she was telling me something personal, something she did not take lightly. It was as though the common experience of astral travel had opened up a new, more personal channel between us. I held her gaze for several seconds.

"You came to me in a dream last night," I told her.

She grabbed her pad and pen. "Tell me about it."

"You told me you had something for me from my grandmother."

She looked at me. "I don't know your grandmother, do I? I only know your aunt."

"No. I doubt you knew my grandmother. She did live in Menlo Park in the 1960s, but I think you were referring to a metaphorical grandmother."

"How so?"

"Do you know anything about Gurdjieff? He wrote a trilogy call *Beelzebub's Tales to His Grandson*."

"Yes, I know of the work. How do I get to know your metaphorical grandmother from that?"

I told her how Gurdjieff's work and personal history had affected me before saying, "His death happened nine months before my birth. I don't think you were seeing another being in me the last time I was here. I did not experience someone taking over my body. I think you were seeing me as I appeared to you in my past life as Gurdjieff."

"You do? Do you remember me from then?"

"Not exactly, but I remember that you told me your age last time."

"Yes, I'm fifty-five."

"Born in 1927, right?"

"Yes, March of that year."

"Gurdjieff's wife died nine months before that date," I told her. I had learned about her death in the book by Peters. "It was a slow death—cancer. Gurdjieff worked very hard to try to cure her and prolong her life."

As I looked at Ruth her face took on a glow and then its features disappeared, replaced by a bright light. I felt a profound connection to her being, not her physical one, but her mental one. I stood up and held open my arms. She put down her pad and pen and embraced me without words.

After a few moments we separated and I sat back down in the patient chair. "So what do you think about my situation with Castaneda and his gang?" I asked.

"Tell me how you feel first."

"Well, after we parted ways the first time I felt elated. I didn't need them or want to be around them. I thought the exchange we had was clearing the air and setting the record straight for me. I was ridding myself from Castaneda's influence for good... but then the astral incident changed that. Do you think I have some more karma to work out with him?"

"I don't know. You may well have."

"I'm kind of nervous about going to places now. In his books Castaneda mentions worthy enemies that sorcerers engage with to test and prove themselves. I'm feeling like I might have fallen into that category. It's scary."

Ruth nodded. "You don't have other family here, do you? I mean, other than your aunt and uncle."

"No. The rest of the family lives in Pennsylvania."

"You haven't found a job. It's been what? Four, five months?"

"Five."

"Maybe it's time to say goodbye to California."

I nodded.

Her words rang true. I should return to where I had a better support system and the cost of living proved more affordable, and a place where I wouldn't have to worry about running into the Carlos gang, at least on the physical plane.

I thanked her and we hugged again. I felt deep respect and gratitude for what she had done for me. The apparition of an old man that she perceived the first time I sat in her chair catapulted me into a series of life-altering experiences. Maybe it was repayment of a karmic debt she owed me for my efforts to help her in our past life together, but whatever the reason, it changed my life forever.

# Chapter 25

*July 1982, Rural Perry County, PA*

"Look, I solved it," I said in a playful way as I handed the Rubik's cube with each side a solid color to my wife.

"Oh, wow!" my wife gushed, dutifully impressed.

"He cheated," my mother-in-law chided from the kitchen.

"What? Did you take off the little colored plastic things and put them back on so they all matched?" my wife asked me.

"No," I said, with a fake smile.

"He took it apart," Meryl's mother told her.

"Yeah, they come apart pretty easily," I confessed. I walked away feeling guilty for taking the easy way. I'd always prided myself in my puzzle solving ability, but after spending hours on the cryptic cube I gave in to frustration and figured out the easier solution. So now, deflated, I sat down in the living room. With a dozen random twists, I scrambled the cube, and thought for a bit. Then I went to a drawer in the cupboard in the study, took out a piece of paper and pencil, and returned. About four-and-a-half hours later I finally solved the cube without resorting to cheating. When I finished I showed my wife.

"This time I didn't cheat," I said as I handed her the cube. "I'm tired. I'm going to bed."

I'd worked many hard hours in the garden that day, and then spent the whole evening after supper working on the mental problem of the cube. I figured that sleep would come without a problem. However, I first wanted to meditate for a bit, per my normal routine.

I sat on a mat on the floor, closed my eyes, and took long, slow breaths. On my third exhalation I felt a slow spinning sensation. I opened my eyes and saw the room from a vantage point outside my body spinning faster and faster until my consciousness flew out of the window in my astral body.

I'm not sure what determines where you go during astral travel, but it seems to depend upon unfinished emotional business. I might have tried to sever my mental connection to Castaneda during our physical encounter two months prior, but the subsequent astral meeting captured my emotional core enough to make me move. On this first astral trip since moving back to Pennsylvania I went directly to that group.

When my travel stopped, I found myself in a medium-sized room with no furnishings and paint peeling off bare walls. A single light bulb dangled from a loose wire in the middle of the room, providing a harsh glaring light that made it hard for me to see anything for a brief second. After a moment, I saw five men.

In addition to my astral visit to the park a couple of months earlier, my prior astral travel included a few short, uneventful trips to local venues or former residences where I had some lingering connections. From these experiences I knew that when traveling in the astral form you can meet other beings, which may also be in astral form, or you might encounter physical beings. You can tell beings in astral form because they do not have the same gravitational influences as a physical body. I could tell that the men on this astral trip had corporeal bodies. The Earth's gravity bound their physical bodies in the normal way, as opposed to my form, which floated in the room.

For a physical entity to interact with an astral form an emotional bond of some sort must exist between the two. I recognized these men from my previous encounters. Their reaction indicated that they knew me, too. I looked at them to gauge the situation. None of the men showed any signs of hostility toward me. The leader, who I recognized in our first meeting as Carlos Castaneda, moved toward me.

"We missed you last night," he said with a broad smile.

I questioned myself. *Last night? This meeting occurs nightly? Were they expecting someone else whom they saw in this manner before?* Then I forced myself to ignore the statement and the questions it engendered and simply focus on my surroundings. From my limited experience in astral travel I knew that things said and heard on the astral plane often had subtle and misconstrued meanings. I couldn't let the statement distract me because I knew that doubt usually terminated an astral experience. I wanted to stay there and get a definitive understanding about this group's attitude toward me.

My mind tried to deal with the contradiction of the apparent friendliness of the group's leader and the previous encounter, which seemed confrontational. Without forming a complete question in my mind I found myself saying, "What about..." I started, but didn't finish.

The doubt in my two words produced a look of apprehension on the faces of all the members of the group and they started to back away. My sudden appearance and my suspicious attitude toward the men must have come across as too aggressive or threatening. The group shifted out of focus for me, and I sensed that I was about to make a hasty exit. In my past astral travel the loss of focus preceded an instant, undesired return to the body. I fought for control. I wanted the encounter to continue.

In an effort to keep them from backing away I attempted to communicate something positive. However, I could not simply talk. Speaking and hearing in astral form don't work in a normal way. I had no physical body to speak with and I did not understand how to control the astral one. I thought of how I could show friendship. Again, without really knowing how, I spoke. I heard myself say, "I really love playing the piano," surprising myself as much as anyone with the statement.

The leader took a step forward again, back to his former spot. "Maybe you can be my opening act," he said.

I remembered the glib retorts this person had given me during our first encounter, so the rather bizarre response to my piano statement didn't faze me. However, the tone of the gathering flipped with the leader of the group now showing the dominant attitude. I felt repulsed. Not because of fear, but because I held no interest in being subordinate, a "second act," to this man. It did seem as though he wanted me as an apprentice of some sort.

Although I didn't want to be a follower, I did not want to drive away the man in front of me. I wanted to understand what led them to me on our first encounter. Did he experience the thought exchange, too? What was the Gurdjieff connection? What goals did they have in that original meeting? What did they want now? Words failed me.

I thought about what I had said when I first realized his identity and his connection to the Golden Eagle. I tried to tell him this again, but instead of saying, "I really enjoyed the eagle's gift," I heard myself say, "I thought the eagle's gift was the Bible."

"What was that?" the man responded, surprised by my remark.

My tone was more obsequious than I intended, but it kept them engaged so I attempted to repeat what I said. To my amazement, I heard myself say the phrase again.

The man puffed out his chest. "Yes, Carlos is very strong," he said as he gave another broad smile.

I looked at him for a second, letting the word "Carlos" sink in. Any doubts I had about his identity disappeared.

As he stood there letting his ego shine, I felt a smile cross my face. Again, without knowing how it happened, I spoke my thoughts. "Yes, but I'm the one who flew to see you."

His chest deflated, but he kept the smile. We exchanged a mutual grin for a few seconds. My mind went back to our previous enigmatic encounters, but before I could ask Carlos his motive for appearing at our first encounter, an urgent fear gripped me. It felt like I needed to get back to my body. During astral travel the heart stops beating and breathing ceases. That only gives you a few short minutes of travel before you must get back to your body, but I didn't understand the mechanics of it.

In all of my previous astral traveling I'd spontaneously returned to my body. I assumed that it always worked that way, but when I wanted to and could not think about anything else, I wasn't able to do it. I felt myself move back from the group as I tried to find the right channel or the right thought to enable my return. Without thinking I opened my mouth, but only a choking sound came out. My form lunged forward.

The blond man's voice broke the tentative silence. "You're dead," he said. His voice carried sarcastic amusement. Carlos held up his hand in a halting gesture. I felt reassured that they would not cause me harm, but I still needed to return to my body. I struggled for the passageway again.

My mouth opened again, and this time a "*Pl*" sound emerged.

Still nothing.

Then finally, without realizing how it happened, in an instant I was back in the bedroom sitting on my mat.

# Chapter 26

*February 1983, Rural Perry County, PA*

In the winter of 1983, more than a year after I quit my job as an electronics technician and took my family to California, I was still unemployed. We lived rent-free in a house owned by my sister. Meryl took a position in retail sales to put food on the table. She didn't relish this low-paying work, and it made me feel inadequate and caused a strain in our relationship.

In winters I often find it challenging to keep a positive outlook, due to the reduced amount of sunlight. This winter, optimism came especially hard. Ten months after my return from California, I stood staring out a bedroom window at the leafless trees, feeling the most depressed I'd ever felt, when a fleeting vision of a building came to me. I recognized it as the location of an electronics manufacturing company, close to the plant where I'd worked as an electronics technician almost a year and a half earlier.

I had only ever experienced such a vision with wide open eyes once before—the golden eagle. The aftermath of this vision proved less traumatic, but equally life changing. The reason I saw this building seemed simple. I needed a job. That place required workers with my skills. The next day I visited the business and applied for work. They had an opening that wasn't even advertised yet. It was for a second-shift supervisor of the production line in the final finish, clean room. I got the job.

My division created crystal timing devices for computers. Each device contained a round piece of quartz very close to the size and thickness of a dime. My workers got the rough-cut stone pieces from the Cutting/Grinding section and applied the final touches. They sorted them, etched them with acid, placed them in metal templates or masks, glued them to wire mounts, stuck them in vacuum machines that applied gold and other precious metals, and finally put stainless steel cases over them.

Working as a supervisor required me to move around a half dozen work stations to observe and interact with over a dozen workers. Occasionally I used the technical skills that got me the job to troubleshoot a machine that malfunctioned, but most of the time the equipment ran without a hitch. At each of these stations I had the option of assisting in the task at hand, all of them tedious in the sense that they required a repetitive non-strenuous motion. Most supervisors only helped whenever a worker did not show up, but I routinely pitched in, creating camaraderie and vaulting my shift's production to the highest in the plant, even though we were second shift and "expected" to do less work than first shift based on historical data.

I found this type of work well suited for living in the moment. I never stayed long enough at a task to tire physically or mentally of the job. I always kept moving on to "make the rounds." I got to a point where I would operate on what seemed like autopilot. I would be sorting some tiny cases into trays or loading a base-plate mask with my mind focused only on the chore. No inner dialogue intruded. When I completed a section, a tray, or a mask, whatever the task, I would move on to the next station. I kept a high energy level throughout the work day.

Since my shift started at 3:30 in the afternoon, I had the mornings free. I spent much of this time with my wife and young children, which now numbered three, as my daughter Joy was born during my time at this job. The children, Meryl, and I had settled into a typical, stable family unit, similar to most in our culture with some exceptions. We didn't have a television and we kept a strict diet, which included as much organic food as possible and no red meat. Our earlier joint interest in spiritual matters had faded somewhat, but I did make an effort to spend quiet time by myself each day.

During my meditations I would engage in techniques I had picked up through my yoga practices and personal experimentation. Patanjali lists faith, high energy, memory, and high intelligence as ingredients needed to achieve astral travel. As I honed these traits to a high degree, the end result came in my ability to control my astral self so that I could leave my physical body and explore the world as an astral being.

I didn't worry about losing control due to my yoga practices, as happened at SKY Land years before, because I did these astral excursions while fully engaged in society. I felt a very strong connection to "reality." I didn't broadcast my new ability either. "Keep your yoga experiences secret," one of my yoga teachers counseled. I followed his advice. I boasted my astral prowess to nobody, including my wife.

# Chapter 27

*October 1985, Rural Perry County, PA*

When I learned how to travel in my astral body I didn't think about how this could physically transpire or how such an entity could have evolved in man, although much later I wrestled with these problems. I simply learned how to acquire the ability to manipulate the astral body, just as a baby learns how to walk.

I would sit in meditation and watch my breath, my prana. As the breath went in and out and the meditation grew deeper, my body relaxed. My respiration became slower and slower. My heart rate dropped, lower and lower until... Finally, my breathing stopped. My heart quit beating. Then my prana would rise without the aid of the diaphragm. I could feel it as I willed it up inside of me from the depths of my being, and when it reached a certain point, a certain chakra, my astral self would escape physical bondage and travel.

I learned to control the travel by learning to control my emotions, since emotions and desire dictate where your astral form goes. The more I developed these powers the more simple my desire became. I no longer desired to meet with the Carlos gang. My last meeting with them had left me satisfied that we should part ways. Instead I wanted to understand the astral mechanism as much as possible. This wish led me to a better understanding of the world in which my astral body traveled.

The most enlightening experience came one day when I left my body and just hung out around my house. We lived in a wooded area about a quarter-mile from any public road at the end of an isolated lane. On that early fall day I floated around, in and out of the house, and around the yard. I even went back to the room where my physical body sat motionless. From this experience I knew that the astral world did not exist as a mysterious place "out there" in a different dimension, as some have argued. Rather, the astral plane overlaps the physical plane in the same way the gravitational field of the sun overlaps the gravitational field of the Earth. This was consistent with the idea that the astral body fell under the influence of the sun's gravitational field and not the Earth's.

The day after I navigated my astral form around my house and yard, I sat in a lotus pose on a sunny spot on my front porch. With my wife and children off for a visit I didn't have to stay in the bedroom to meditate, but could enjoy the fresh air and sunshine during my daily practices. As I drifted deep into meditation I initiated the familiar sequence of breathing and mental exercises that led to release of my astral form.

Just as I started the final step of using the center of my will to force the prana to rise, I felt a pang of guilt. The process halted. Why the crisis of conscience? As I pondered the meaning of the guilty feeling I came to a realization. Astral travel no longer held any purpose for me. When I ventured into astral form in the past I never questioned a purpose. I simply wanted to experience it, and so I did. My desire for the experience was enough.

But now I had lost that desire. I knew how to make astral travel occur and where I could go when I did. The mystery was gone. With this acknowledgment of loss of curiosity also came the realization that such activity jeopardized my ability to provide as a father and husband since the action involved risks. In order to leave my physical body my heartbeat stopped. I'd read in some esoteric work that astral travel could lead to death. I already encountered one close call with Castaneda's gang.

To continue traveling outside my body without a purpose entailed recklessness. As I finished my meditation session for the day I knew that the quest to understand my spiritual nature was complete and the seeking days of my youth past, eclipsed by my quest to become a provider for my family in the physical world.

Even if I hadn't made a conscious decision to stop leaving my physical body, I believe I would have soon lacked the ability to do so. Astral travel requires knowledge of proper technique, plus a balanced body and a balanced mind. Your right brain and left brain need to work together and not have one dominating the other. I lost that equilibrium.

My job as supervisor did not require much reading and writing. I had a minimum of paperwork. Doing this minimal amount of language-associated mental work kept my body balanced and made astral travel feasible. Soon after I decided to stop the practice, my company lost its contract with IBM. They laid me off, and after some time as a security guard working the night shift, my karma led me into the left-brain dominated world of academia that I have inhabited ever since. I believe that anyone whose left brain dominates the right will find it difficult to achieve astral travel.[1]

---

[1] I am aware that many people consider astral travel an easier task than I portray. If you do an internet search you can find several websites that offer ways you can learn how to astral travel. These methods don't indicate stopping the heart. I suggest that what they are doing is traveling in the phantom body rather than the astral body. You can see a broader discussion of this topic on my website:
www.holisticemotivepractices.com\presentations\
Spirit%20Bodies%20and%20Beyond.pdf

# Chapter 28

*July 1988, Middletown, PA*

I took my yellow 1976 Opel Manta out of gear, turned the switch on, but didn't engage the starter. No use. The starter hadn't worked for several months and I hadn't located one in any junkyard. Instead I opened the driver's door, stepped out, and with one hand on the steering wheel pushed the vehicle forward until it started to roll down the slight grade. When the car picked up speed I hopped in, popped the clutch, and drove off to my eight o'clock class in Experimental Psychology at Penn State's Capital campus.

Maybe I didn't have the resources to buy another car, but I could afford to go back to college. My three years of college credits and four years of experience in electronics had qualified me to teach at Thomson Institute in their Associate's degree program in Electronics Technology. After teaching during the day for two years I switched to the newly created night program in order to take classes at Penn State. My employer provided me $200 per class toward tuition, while Lehigh University gave me a grant that covered full tuition for the Penn State classes.

"I never heard of a school paying someone to go to another school," I told the financial aid officer at Lehigh. I'd contacted them out of desperation after being turned down for aid at Penn State.

"This is all new to us, too," the woman had told me, as she awarded me the grant. I couldn't believe my luck. I was actually making $200 by attending each class. It would only take three semesters to finish my bachelor's degree.

From a student's perspective an eight o'clock class is something to be avoided at all costs, but I needed Experimental Psych if I wanted to complete my Lehigh degree with a psychology major and it was only offered at 8:00 A.M. At first it seemed like an impossible situation. I lived sixty miles away and taught night school from 6:00–10:30 P.M., which meant getting home later than 11:30 P.M. But getting to my eight o'clock turned out to be easy. I found a private campground halfway between Penn State's Capital campus and where I taught. After I dismissed my last class I drove the five miles to the campground, put my $12.00 into the late arrival box, and pitched my tent. I made sure I parked on a slope with the front end facing down the grade.

As the oldest student in Dr. Peters's class I felt a little self-conscious at first. I was even older than the professor. But any feelings of insecurity soon evaporated as it became clear that my focus and drive put me at an advantage over the majority of my younger classmates. Many seemed to lack ambition, like I had at their age. They only wanted to do as much as necessary to get through each class. By the middle of the six-week summer term I felt relaxed and confident. My journey back into the academic world looked promising.

Some of that confidence, however, was jolted one particular day. Toward the end of a class about which statistical tests to use in an experimental design, a young student raised his hand.

"Yes, George?" Dr. Peters's voice showed signs of irritation. George had a penchant for not keeping focused on the topic at hand.

"Do any psychologists believe in reincarnation?"

Dr. Peters, who had been writing on the board, dropped his hand to his side. "Where do you come up with these questions?"

"I don't know." George gave his characteristic self-conscious laugh before he re-asked, "Do they?"

Dr. Peters gave George a petulant look. "Only the tragically chic," he answered before continuing to talk about regression analysis.

The exchange gave me pause. I had never spoken to anyone other than my wife and Ruth Estes about my feelings concerning reincarnation. I wondered whether I would ever talk to another person about reincarnation, or if I would keep repressing the thoughts until someday they would disappear.

Academia didn't seem ready for my experiences with reincarnation and astral travel, and if I had to choose between academia and my past, it seemed obvious that I needed to keep pushing forward toward Tufts.

# Chapter 29

*February 1989, Somerville, MA*

The Bollywood music coming through the speakers in the ceiling, the Hindu paintings and sculptures, and the smell of curry and masala created an atmosphere that took me back to the Kripalu Ashram. I recalled the experience with chanting there and how it resulted in my quest to understand the impact of sounds on emotions. Ultimately that experience brought me to this restaurant in Davis Square, just a few blocks from the Tufts University Somerville campus.

After the waiter took our orders, the Tufts psychology professor seated across from me spoke. "Well, first of all, I want to let you know that you have been accepted into the program." Our outing to the Indian restaurant was part of my visit to Tufts as a prospective graduate student. "That should take a little tension out of our conversation."

"Good. Yes, I should say." I relaxed as I sat back in my chair and cracked a wistful smile. "And I made it before my hair turned gray."

"Well, I must say we don't consider hair color when evaluating applicants." He returned my smile as he took a sip of water.

"Your qualifications are top notch, but I suppose you will be one of the oldest students to go through the program." He put the glass down before continuing. "That could be to your advantage. You have more life experience."

He paused, and when I just nodded he spoke again. "So what have your recent experiences been? I did read them on your application, I'm sure, but I've read quite a few lately."

"For the past three years I've been teaching computer electronics in a post-secondary school."

"Well, that should have you ready to plow into serious studying."

"Yes," I said. "I believe I'm ready. Now if it would have been three years ago, it would have been a different story."

"Oh, really? Why is that?"

"Since I hadn't done any serious studying for some time, the first weeks I taught required enormous effort to regain my ability to process written language, especially technical language. I had to read, and reread, each passage before I could digest the content."

"Yes, it is amazing how the brain works like other parts of the body. If you don't use it on a regular basis, it gets lazy and forgets how to work."

"Yes, but after a few weeks I adjusted," I said. "In my second year I switched to teaching nights so I could take courses to finish my bachelor's degree."

"So you just got your bachelor's?" he sounded surprised. "You have a family, too, don't you?"

"Yes, a wife and three kids."

"That took some drive, working and going to college at the same time," he said.

I shrugged my shoulders, uncomfortable with the compliment. "I guess so."

For the rest of the meal the professor talked about his work. In academia, at least at major universities like Tufts, all professors have a line of study. In Tufts's psych department everyone pursued investigations into some experimental area of psychology. In order for grad students to succeed they must find a mentor whose work interests them and get under his or her wing, so to speak. In short, a new grad student needs to search out someone he feels comfortable with and who is willing to take him or her on.

On the other side of the grad student–prof equation sits the professor. The tenure committee wants to see that his or her program of study can attract students and guide them in the production of work worthy of a doctorate degree. At the outset of my trip to Tufts I knew about the first half of the equation—that I had to find a mentor. With the free meal and flattery at Namaskar on Davis Square I found out about the other half.

On my application to Tufts I had to choose what general field of psychology I wanted as my major. I had four choices: developmental, social, physiological, and cognitive. I listed cognitive. The department had three people whose work fell under the cognitive psychology umbrella. My host for the meal announced to me, with some obvious pleasure, that he had persuaded the other two cognitive psych profs that he should have "first dibs" on me, as he put it.

As I dined on chicken vindaloo, the professor introduced me to his field of study. I listened politely, but with little interest. His program sounded uninspiring. It had something to do with the way decisions are made. I nodded a lot and smiled, but felt uncomfortable at being courted in such a manner.

The next day I met with a second cognitive psychology professor in his office. He also tried to impress me with his work, which involved mathematical modeling of psychological processes, a hot field at the time and one that I found interesting, but not drawn to. He seemed less pushy about his work, though.

"I just want to let you know that you have the opportunity to do mathematical modeling here at Tufts, if that is what you desire," he said in a matter-of-fact manner. I surmised that his nonchalant approach had something to do with his tenured status.

The third Tufts cognitive psychologist happened to be in San Diego at the time of my visit, so I didn't get a chance to talk with him. However, part of the itinerary of the trip included talking with current grad students, and I visited with one of his students.

"So what's your area of interest?" Stan asked after I introduced myself.

"I'm interested in how the brain processes language." I didn't get into specifics about my desire to understand the link between sounds and emotions or how one might use sounds to affect emotional state, as accomplished through chanting.

"Oh, really?" he replied. "So am I. In fact, I'm just working on finishing up my dissertation in psycholinguistics. I just have a few changes to make. I'm supposed to be done by next week." His voice showed signs of weariness.

"Oh, really?"

"Yes, I was supposed to start a post doc a couple of weeks ago, but I got the position postponed for a month."

"Oh. So what's the topic of your dissertation?" I asked.

He went into some details of his work on how the brain processed syntax in language. His use of biofeedback equipment to measure brain waves caught my attention. In my efforts to educate myself about language and emotions I had read a brief account of a study on brain waves recorded while listening to speech sounds.

"That seems along the lines of what I'd like to pursue. Who is your advisor?" I asked.

He told me his advisor's name and then added, "You should meet him. I think you would like him. He is great to work with."

When he said this to me, I perceived a change in his appearance. His face and the area surrounding his head went slightly out of focus and took on a shimmering and wavy aspect, as if a sudden heat had somehow filled the surrounding air. At the same time I felt a strong feeling of trust and companionship with him. At that instant I knew my choice of graduate advisors, even though I hadn't had a chance to meet him.

I had experienced this kind of unusual perception on several prior occasions. One of those times occurred in a conversation with a Mormon missionary. I don't remember the topic of conversation at the time, only that he had expressed a point of view and that I felt support for it. The missionary told me at that time, *"What you are seeing and feeling is the Holy Spirit."* Apparently he had the same altered perception, and not for the first time, since he identified the experience.

When Ruth Este told me she saw me as an old man, I saw her image distort in a way similar to what I saw in Stan and with the missionary, although in a more pronounced state. The image of her face started out as only wavy, but then, instead of just a wavy distortion, I saw Ruth as a caricature, first of a clown and then of a squirrel, while she saw me as an old man and young woman.

I believe that anyone who dismisses what I saw with Stan, the missionary, and Ruth as illusions or hallucinations makes a mistake. The odds of simultaneous hallucinations would strike me as more farfetched than the probability that some kind of shared physical basis lies behind the phenomena. They were simultaneous with Ruth and the missionaries, though I never asked Stan whether he had an unusual perception when I did.

I cannot fathom the nature of the physical processes that happen whenever these altered perceptions occur. It might involve quantum gravitational influences causing a perception distortion. Perhaps these influences occur in such a way that the higher bodies directly communicate or interact in some manner. This seems like a plausible explanation, given the nature of the distortion that Ruth Este saw in my appearance.

That summer, after feeling good about my acceptance into the Tufts graduate psychology program, a grim financial reality set in. We lost a car in a flash flood. Rather, my wife lost a car. This happened, she told me, while she drove home from her mother's with our two oldest children. The pouring rain covered the road in the flats as she approached our village. Just after she crossed the bridge over the little creek on the edge of town the car stalled as the water covered the engine.

"Don't panic," she told the children. Then she calmly rolled down the window and let out a yell at the top of her voice, "Help!"

When nobody magically appeared out of the darkness, she methodically got out of the driver's window leg first and opened the back window in the nearly waist deep water. She led our seven-year-old son out and held his hand while gathering our four-year-old daughter into her other arm and onto her hip, and they waded in the swift flowing water the thirty or so yards to higher ground. Meryl, Aaron and Adia were lucky to have escaped without any physical harm, but the emotional trauma did leave a scar. For years Adia would express fear and close her eyes when traveling over a bridge in a car.

Insurance never pays enough to cover the entire loss. Besides, our tiny Fiesta had so little value that the pittance we received in compensation didn't begin to cover a down payment for a serviceable used vehicle. Although I earned enough from teaching electronics to pay my bills, I had no cash reserves. After looking into the possibility of renting in the Boston area I didn't see how I could come up with the nearly two thousand dollars I would need for a month's rent plus a security deposit.

Faced with the new expense of replacing a car, the knowledge of the cost of renting in Boston, and the fact that graduate student stipends don't go far enough for a single grad student, I had no choice but to ask Tufts for a year's extension on my matriculation and pray for a miracle to later allow me to be able to afford a chance to realize my dream of becoming a Tufts grad student.

# CHAPTER 30

*August 1989, Ickesburg, PA*

"I don't know if you know it or not, but your shed is on fire."

I didn't even respond to my neighbor's voice. I slammed the receiver back upon the wall and dashed to my car. By the time I drove the twenty minutes from my father's house to my home, only smoke remained, billowing out from under the remnants of the roof of the two-story structure. The local volunteer firemen had the blaze under control, but I could see the damage. The corner of the house closest to the building appeared charred and the shed itself looked totally lost.

Without a doubt the boys who confessed to starting the blaze suffered when their parents learned of their deed. The parents themselves suffered when the insurance company stuck them with the bill for damages. However, this apparent tragedy resulted in a blessing for me. With the nearly one-half year of my current salary in insurance money, the final piece to get me to the program of my desires had fallen into place, eight years after I first pointed to the Tufts page in the library.

*January 1990, Medford, MA*

I quit my teaching job in January, left my family behind, and headed to Boston to prepare for graduate school in the expensive Boston suburbs. Although leaving my family was difficult, I knew from the experience at the library that I was doing the right thing. My plan was to find a good place for us to live, and then bring the rest of the family to join me in June after the school year was over. Meryl was excited and happy for me to be able to attain my goal. My children, too, were all excited. They were going to get to live in the Boston area. I found it amazing that young children—eleven, eight, and five years old at the time—felt the allure of a big city. Maybe it was just something new, an adventure that they yearned for, but at any rate they couldn't wait to head for "the Hub of New England."

Although I wouldn't enroll until the fall semester, I needed time to get settled in and January was a good time to find a temporary apartment in an area with so many colleges starting a new semester. I did no planning before I left early in the morning, two days before Tufts's spring semester began. When I reached campus, I went to the psychology department and asked if they knew anyone I might stay with for a day or two while I looked for an apartment. A grad student present at the time offered me space on his living room floor. The next day I answered an ad for a roommate and moved in with two other grad students.

I knew that I would need to work nights in order to afford the cost of living in Boston. It took about six weeks to land an electronics teaching position similar to the one I'd left in Pennsylvania. When June approached I found a spacious apartment, the top two stories of an old Victorian house, about three miles from Tufts's campus. The week after school ended, I rented a Ryder truck, and with the help of my father and stepmother and some of my new electronics students, we moved our belongings into our new home. My children each had their own bedroom. I had a separate room for my computer and desk. The excitement ran high for my children, my wife, and me. A dream was coming true for all of us.

After I moved to the Boston area and before my fall classes started, I spent a great deal of time in the Boston Public Library. A year earlier, James Gleick's best-selling book, *Chaos: Making a New Science*, piqued my interest in chaos theory. When I learned that mathematical equations could describe complex systems that look chaotic, it seemed like an important discovery, something almost mystical, but rational at the same time.

One day while looking for other work on the topic, a book came off of the shelf with an energy that reminded me how the linguistics book popped into my hands almost a decade earlier. In this book, *Order Out of Chaos*, Ilya Prigogine, a Nobel prize winner in the field of chemistry, and co-author Isabelle Stengers presented many details concerning the equilibrium of complex chemical systems. The point that I found most interesting dealt with gravity and complex systems.

The authors claimed that in complex chaotic systems, gravity plays a more important role than previously thought. This led me to a series of internal questions with the possibility of some profound answers. What effect does gravity have on the most complex system in nature, the human nervous system, including primarily the brain? Do the gravitational forces of distant bodies have a significant influence? The text appeared to suggest this. Can a human learn how to control this force and separate the various gravitational influences? This must be what occurs in those who have learned astral travel.

My hunch about gravity playing a role in reincarnation and astral body experiences found some important backing with this theory. This corroboration of an old idea awakened a part of me that lay dormant. I last traveled in my astral body over four years earlier. Thoughts about those experiences, buried deep in my mind, came back with this book. It gave me hope of reaching a better understanding of what caused those experiences.

## *October 1990, Medford, MA*

Less than a year later I managed to discuss Prigogine's claims with one of the nation's premier philosophers, Daniel Dennett. As a student in Professor Dennett's Philosophy of Mind class I listened intently to all of his lectures. One day in the middle of the semester he put on the blackboard a series of four terms with arrows connecting them, in this manner.

Chaos → Order → Life → Intelligence.

"We can identify four distinct stages in the evolution of the mind," he told the class.

"Of course, it all started with chaos. Cosmologists agree that the initial stage of the universe consisted of no identifiable pattern. No organization. Exactly the definition of chaos. Somehow, and it's not really clear how—perhaps through random chance, but certainly following the laws of physics—chaos was supplanted by order. Molecules were formed. Simple ones at first. Then more complex ones. Then eventually, over millennia, the proper sequences of these ordered molecules came together to foster life. Simple life at first, but then, through natural selection, intelligence ultimately developed."

A student raised her hand. "So, you are saying that intelligence is basically the result of natural selection?" she asked.

"That's right. Once life was established, intelligence is the logical conclusion of the natural selection process."

"And we don't have much of a clue about how life itself came about?"

"Life seems to have formed from a process of more or less random combinations of molecules. We don't really know how the molecules themselves first appeared."

After the class I gathered my papers and rushed out after Dennett. I caught up with him in the stairwell.

"Professor Dennett," I said, trying not to sound too excited.

"Yes?"

"I was wondering... You know when you talked about the step between order and chaos?"

"Yes."

"Well, I was wondering if you are familiar with what Prigogine has written on that topic."

He paused a moment before forming a response. "Yes, I am," he said. "I have thought about what he has said, but you know, it just opens it up to the occult," he concluded with a slight shake of his head.

My jaw dropped. I wasn't ready for a dismissal of Prigogine's idea about the influence of gravity on complex systems because of the conclusions it might lead to. I wanted to discuss its empirical merits. When I didn't reply to his statement, Professor Dennett turned and continued down the steps. I stood still in the stairwell for a few seconds registering my disappointment. The academic door to the mysteries of reincarnation and astral travel appeared locked, and I doubted if anyone wanted to find the key.

# Chapter 31

*November 1990, Somerville, MA*

    I found my time attending grad school at Tufts the most exhilarating period of my life. I relished the challenge of proving my worth as a psychologist. If the professor assigned a ten-page paper, I found myself writing a twenty-page one. In addition, the Boston area afforded our family many cultural opportunities. All the children loved the museums and I got to take my wife to Symphony Hall to hear flutist Jean-Pierre Rampal, her idol ever since she was a flute major in college. With three children and the excitement of the city, the spiritual experiences of prior years began to fade. Meryl and I didn't practice yoga together anymore, although I still did yoga postures on a daily basis, but more for the physical benefit than any spiritual component.

    At forty, I was the oldest of all students in the Tufts graduate psychology program. Even though I was about fifteen years above the median age, there were a couple of students in their thirties with whom I formed good friendships, including Jan, an energetic, tall woman who had danced professionally in her twenties. When the legs and beauty of youth turned thirty, she decided to go back to school.

    "I thought emotions were akin to the third rail of psychology," I told her when I learned she was studying emotional development. "At least that's what I've been advised," I said, trying to talk over the din of the other students and the clanging of trays being deposited into the return slots in the student dining area.

    "Really?" Jan sounded unconvinced as she chewed another bite of salad.

    "Yeah," I insisted. "I was told you shouldn't be studying them until you have tenure, that is, if you ever want to get tenure. You must not have gotten that memo," I joked.

"Guess not." She finished a couple of more forks of salad while I ate mine, and then added, "Sounds like you want to study emotions, but are just too afraid of getting shunned."

I looked up, a bit surprised at her insight. "Yeah, you can see right through me," I said. "I'm interested in understanding how emotions and language interact."

"So you can't get your advisor to agree to let you pursue that?" she asked.

"Well, I haven't really asked. My advisor's research involves analyzing and interpreting brain activity recorded during language processing and other cognitive tasks. The experimental subjects, that is, undergrad freshmen and sophomores taking Intro to Psych, sit in this sound-proof isolation room with electrodes on their heads. They use a joystick to react to various mental games and puzzles that appear on a computer screen. There really isn't anything emotional involved."

I took a drink of juice and waited for a reaction from Jan. She nodded in agreement, but continued to eat.

I continued, "My initial approach to studying the connection of emotion to sound was to focus on sounds. I figured I can get at the emotional connection in due time. I thought that my master's thesis should entail recording and analyzing brain activity associated with individual language sounds, like single sounds, you know—phonemes, the smallest sound units of spoken language."

"You mean like '*ah*' and '*mm*' and '*rr*'?" she asked.

"That's right. But this would be a huge departure from my advisor's work." My voice betrayed glumness as I pushed around the rejected chickpeas remaining on my otherwise cleaned plate.

"Yeah, it gets risky if you get too far from your advisor's work. He's liable to lose interest in what you're doing," she told me.

"Exactly. He did know of some work on brain waves and phonemes, but after I read the studies and saw how inconclusive they were, I knew I didn't have much chance for success pursuing that line of research. Surface electrodes just don't have the precision necessary to differentiate neural sources of individual phonemes."

Jan nodded again. "It's not like you can place electrodes inside the brains of volunteers from Intro."

I gave an involuntary laugh at the image of placing electrodes in the heads of Tufts students.

"Yeah, I know," I said. "Instead I'm choosing the easier path of basing my thesis on work that's part of my advisor's National Institute of Health grant. It's focused on how language and object recognition work together. Pretty far afield from where I wanted to go, but I'm just being practical."

Jan looked at her watch and stood up. "Speaking of Intro, I have to get to class. I'm a teaching assistant for Professor Davidson this semester."

"I'll walk along. I have to get back to the lab."

We deposited our trays and left the Mayer Campus Center, heading toward Paige Hall. The chilly November air felt invigorating as we strolled through the dead leaves amid a multitude of students hurrying to their next class.

"You're lucky to have a research assistantship," Jan said, as we neared her destination. "I bet that really helps you in getting your thesis work done. I have to do the teaching assistant gig. It's okay, but takes a lot of time. Instead of helping in my research, it makes it harder." Jan sounded down and a bit jealous of my status as a research assistant.

As we said goodbye I thought about my good fortune in obtaining the position of research assistant in my advisor's electrophysiology lab in my first semester at Tufts. Most grad students start out as teaching assistants, and then maybe in their second or third year, if they are lucky enough to have an advisor with grant money, they can become a research assistant. Because my advisor's lab required a high level of technical expertise to run the computers and electrical equipment, my electronics and programming background got me a research position in my first year.

However, I did have one problem that the others didn't have. None of the other grad students in the psych department at Tufts had children. I had three. The financial burden of providing for my family kept me working nights the whole time I studied at Tufts. I taught computer electronics at a technical school four nights a week, four hours a night.

A typical day for me started with teaching my home-schooled son for an hour. Then I rode my bike the four miles through the city to the campus where I worked as a research assistant and attended classes. In the afternoon I rode my bike back to our place in the Oak Grove neighborhood of Malden, ate supper, and afterwards walked four blocks to the subway station. I took the Orange Line to Downtown Crossing then changed to the Red Line and got off at Central Square, Cambridge, where I taught from 6:00 until 10:30 P.M. Afterwards I caught the subway back to Oak Grove and walked home, arriving sometime after 11:30 P.M., exhausted, but not yet done for the day. There was always reading and papers to write. I considered turning in before 1:00 A.M. a good bedtime.

## CHAPTER 32

*February 1991, Somerville, MA*

My desire to understand the relationships between emotions and sounds propelled me to grad school, but because the subject diverged so far from my advisor's expertise, my master's thesis didn't deal with that topic. Fortunately the graduate program allowed students to pursue independent study in a field of his or her choosing. I took advantage of this avenue of learning to expand my knowledge in two areas of interest—linguistics and emotions. Through studying linguistics I incorporated primary consonants into the previously established scheme of three primary vowels. Research into emotions revealed how emotions can be categorized, based on physiology, in a way that fit seamlessly with these primary speech sounds. With this fresh knowledge I tackled my first experiment in search of evidence to support a budding theory of how speech sounds affect emotions.

"Okay, everyone ready?" I asked. I peered inside the sound-attenuated room where three Tufts psych grad students sat on hardback chairs, and a fourth sat in the soft easy chair where subjects for the electrophysiology studies usually sat.

A round of affirmative answers came back and I closed the door and turned on the recorder. "Okay, go ahead. I'm recording," I said through the intercom.

"Rrr."

"Aah."

"Sss."

Gales of laughter erupted from the room. For about the fifth time I turned off the recorder. Group reciting of single sounds into a common microphone in a small 10' x 10' dimly lit room was more fun than I thought it would be. My volunteer friends were enjoying the novel atmosphere and releasing their inhibitions.

This time I didn't open the door, but instead used the intercom. "Okay, let's try it again." I tried not to sound frustrated. I didn't want to offend them. Besides, their laughter was contagious. It was funny to me, too.

"Rrr."

"Aah."

"Sss."

"Mmmmm."

"Whoa, whoa," I said into the intercom. "I don't want emotional inflections. That '*mmm*' was almost seductive. I need your tone of voice to be neutral."

"Okay, sorry," came the reply. Then silence... followed by faint giggles and, "I couldn't help myself."

This was the first psych experiment that I attempted completely on my own. It started with recording the stimuli. For this task I talked four fellow psych grad students into providing voices. I gave the students—two males and two females—a list of sounds and asked them to alternate in reading them while I ran a tape recorder. It may sound simple, but nothing is ever as simple as it sounds.

After two more false starts, my cohorts finally made it through the entire list of sounds. Each of them got to say all of the six sounds four times—ninety-six separate stimuli altogether. The timing I asked them to follow worked out to about two-second intervals between the sounds, so the entire list lasted just over three minutes.

I told my friends that I was conducting an experiment but couldn't tell them about the details before they recorded the sounds because I didn't want to prejudice the way they spoke them.

I wanted to get people to rate the sounds on three dimensions of emotional experience: emotional arousal, emotional pleasantness, and emotional control or power. I picked the six sounds my fellow grad students recorded because my preliminary research led me to believe that these six had special connections to the dimensions of emotion. I predicted that the "*rrr*," as in an aggressive growl, would get rated the most arousing, and that people would rate the "*ahh*," as in "Ah, that feels good," as the least arousing or the most relaxing. The "*mmm*," as in "Mm, mm, good" should get the highest rating on the pleasant scale, and at the other extreme, the least pleasant, or rather, most unpleasant, would be the "*ooh*," like "Ooh, that is gross." The sound corresponding to the most control or most power I felt would be the "*sss*," a very strict sound, and the "*eee*," like a squeal of fright, should be the sound showing the least emotional control.

The next week I herded several groups of eight Tufts undergrads who were taking Introduction to Psychology into a small testing room in the psych building where they listened to the ninety-six sounds and rated them. The course required students to participate in psych experiments. It didn't require them to be enthusiastic or engaged. I didn't see either of those traits in the students who completed my experiment. The only thing they seemed interested in was to make sure their names were on the attendance list so they would get credit for attending.

The next week I sat in front of the computer screen in the basement of the psychology building, hoping to find results that would support my predictions. After tabulating all of the responses I first looked at the ratings on the pleasantness/ unpleasantness scale. *Yes!* I felt a rush of excitement. *The "mmm" sound received the highest pleasantness rating by far.* But my elation subsided when I noted that the average rating of the "ooh" fell on the pleasant side of the rating scale. In fact, no sounds were rated unpleasant. *Were students having a positive bias and just trying to be cooperative?* My disappointment intensified when I looked at the in-control vs. out-of-control scale. The *"eee"* and *"sss"* sounds did not show any hint of what I had expected for this rating measure.

Crestfallen, I continued on to the arousal/relaxation rating. Was there something here that could salvage my research effort? I ran the numbers and then reran them, the second time breaking down the results by gender of the person speaking the sounds. *Well, something interesting, if not exactly what I predicted,* I told myself when I found that students rated the *"rrr"* sounds spoken by males as more arousing, and the *"aah"* sounds spoken by females as more relaxing. The result spoke to gender stereotypes, however, more than it did to my conjecture.

Later that week I sat at my desk in my apartment during a late evening study session pondering the failure of my experiment to corroborate my theory. *Was it the disengagement of the students? Maybe I should have placed individual subjects in a room by themselves and told them to say the sounds and then rate how it made them feel?* I tried to picture how that might work until another stream of thought interrupted. *Or was it the stimuli? Perhaps I should have given my friends different instructions, like "Now try to make these sounds feel relaxing" and "Next try to make these sounds feel out of control."* Then I could see which sound best conveyed a particular feeling.

These were good questions. Ones that I wanted to pursue.

# Chapter 33

*October 1992, Somerville, MA*

If I didn't get the results I wanted for my first foray into experimental work with sounds and emotions, at least I learned something. I learned that coming up with the proper experimental design took more than time and effort. It took insight into a world of complex variables. I needed to understand not just sounds and emotions, but I also needed to know more about psychology and different approaches to experimental methods.

The chance for me to tinker with the design of my first experiment and further my work in this vein didn't happen while I was at Tufts. There never were enough hours in the day, it seemed. My night school teaching job and the Psychology program's course load prohibited further explorations. I did learn quite a bit more about experimental methods there, but through electrophysiology research on language and picture recognition, not research on sounds and emotions.

I felt frustration from failing to advance the research that had compelled me to attend grad school, but I managed to keep my mind focused on advancing my personal knowledge of how sounds interact with emotions. The primary source for this effort came from a book written by a Sufi called *The Ninety-Nine Names of Allah*. This book captured my attention during a visit to the new-age bookstore in Palo Alto. It seemed to have a glowing energy surrounding it, a mystical power that beckoned to me. Although I embraced the Western scientific approach with my matriculation to Tufts, I still had significant emotional connections to the Sufis. I kept this slender volume with the "beautiful names," as the Sufis call them, in my backpack during my first two years at Tufts as I traveled, via public transportation, to and from campus and Central Square in Cambridge where I taught computer electronics at night.

Buses and subway cars offered less than ideal venues for self-study of the impact of mantras. Two problems arose. First, the distractions: traffic noise, subway car noise, people noise. Then there was the "looking weird" factor. The subway already amassed a sufficient collection of strange folks. I didn't need to add to their numbers by sitting with closed eyes, chanting a foreign word. So I opted out of straight up chanting and substituted saying the words under my breath, or only in my mind.

Concurrent with my working with the names, I learned, through independent study, how the physiology of emotions could be categorized on three dimensions and found evidence that matched each primary sound to a distinct dimension of emotion physiology. I grasped what some of the names could do in an emotional sense. Over time, as I tried to see patterns in the names, I came to know each by heart. Grouping the names by their first letter facilitated this. This practice helped me discover the importance of the initial sound of a word when using it for working with emotions. I found that I could affect my emotions only by choosing a word that started with the sound that corresponded to my current emotional state. If I was tired, I couldn't use a name starting with an arousing *"rrr"* sound. I wouldn't have the energy to carry out the plan that such a word would demand. But if it was the start of the day and I was full of energy, then an *"rrr"* word would fit. Which one? I could run the list of *"rrr"* names through my mind and in a flash hear what name would work.

Having spent so much time working with the ninety-nine names made it easy to try them with my newfound awareness of the emotional valence of sounds. During long and trying fourteen-hour days, when I traveled on the subway or sat on a bench waiting for a bus, I would match my mood to a starting sound, pick out an appropriate name, and say it under my breath to provide solace.

"Hhh aaa lll eee mmm."

I would hear the sound in my mind as I exhaled with my back against the subway seat. Eyes still open, mind you. No weirdness, just a little relief from the bustle of the day. The *"Hhh"* expressed the exhaustion I felt, the tiredness. A little relaxing came with the *"aaa."* Then with the *"lll"* I felt a centering effect. The *"eee"* released control, and the *"mmm"* delivered the pleasant finale. *Haleem* made things more bearable.

After realizing the usefulness of the names of Allah I wanted to see if I could apply the sound-emotion relationships to Hindu mantras. I worked with a number of popular ones and did feel some powerful effects, but these only seemed to work in a meditative setting and then only as a way to push me deeper into a feeling of losing myself. When I wanted something that would help me in day-to-day functioning, I turned to the names of Allah. I kept the Hindu and Sanskrit mantras to times of meditation.

I also tried to fashion my own words for mantras as I dealt with feelings throughout the day, but I always found myself debating which sounds to use and ultimately wound up sticking with one of the ninety-nine names, not just because it worked, but also because it eliminated the internal debate. Stopping the dialogue still made sense as a personal goal. Using the names of Allah helped me work through emotional knots and kept me on course, like a rudder steering my ship of feelings.

With the help of mantras I weathered my third year at Tufts in good spirits, but the lengthy days still carried a physical toll. From the start of my studies I knew they considered the Tufts Ph.D. psychology program a five-year program, but when I learned that one student obtained a paying position after finishing her required courses in the third year, I wanted to do the same. Working long days for little pay motivated me to find a job where I could complete my degree and better support my family with a less hectic schedule.

At the end of my third year at Tufts I lined up a junior faculty slot at the University of Arkansas for Medical Sciences. I got assurances from my new employer that I could complete my dissertation work and independent study while doing electrophysiology research in the lab of the person who hired me.

My wife saw the position as progress for my career and she supported the move, although she gave up a position in management at a day care center. With the significant increase in salary I received, she saw it as a step forward for our family. My son couldn't wait to move to Arkansas. The prior two summers Aaron toured the eastern half of the country from Florida to Ontario as part of a drum and bugle corps. For several weeks his corps shared the road with a corps from Arkansas. He already had a number of Arkansas friends. My two daughters were the reluctant ones. Both Adia and Joy complained about leaving their friends and protested the move, but it took less than a week in our new home for them to find a new set of friends.

# Chapter 34

*July 1994, Little Rock, AR*

I gave a tug on the large metal handle, but the door didn't budge. I gave a harder pull, throwing my weight into it, and the copper flanges on the door jerked apart from the flanges on the frame. I peered inside the brightly lit room. The space was more than twice as large as the sound-proof testing booth at Tufts and was decorated with bright pictures of Barney, Big Bird, and the rest of Sesame Street on the wall. It boasted a festive atmosphere compared to the dungeon-like lab where I'd worked for three years prior to coming to Arkansas Children's Hospital.

*If only the stupid door would be easier to open,* I thought. Located in a hospital, the electrophysiology recording room had to be electronically isolated from possible MRI (Magnetic Resonance Imaging) interference. The whole room was lined with copper and a large copper cable led to an outside ground. The copper on the door meshed so tightly with the copper on the doorframe that a regular pull would net nothing. For most people it took a hard two-handed yank.

"How's it going?" I asked Linda, the lab technician.

"Oh, we're just about ready," she replied. She continued applying conductive gel into the electrodes that studded the elastic cap on the child's head. "Only three more to go."

"Okay, good."

I closed the door, lightly this time, and went over and sat down in front of the computer that was hooked up to the bank of biomedical amplifiers that were connected to the electrodes attached to the child. I started the test program and eighteen traces of recordings appeared running across the screen. One trace showed galvanized skin response (GSR), which detected changes in perspiration. GSR is used in lie detection. Your palms and other areas of skin tend to get sweaty whenever you feel guilty. Another trace displayed electrocardiogram (EKG), a measure of the heartbeat, and sixteen traces presented electroencephalogram (EEG), a record of brain activity. When the traces reached the right-hand side of the screen, they started back at the left, overwriting the previous recording. I watched, looking for any potential problems.

After a minute or two Linda stuck her head out of the room. "All done," she announced.

"The data looks clean," I said. "We can get started."

Linda went back into the room and smiled at the sixth grader sitting in the soft, over-stuffed chair.

"Okay, the first thing we're going to do is have you listen to some sounds. There are going be sounds of people saying things like '*aah*,' '*ooo*' and '*eee*'," she told the subject. "You don't have to do anything. Just try to sit still and try not to blink too much. Just listen."

"Okay."

Linda closed the door tightly behind her, walked over to the command computer, and started the experimental protocol.

I let Linda run the whole thing. As a paid technician, that was part of her job, but I had a lot invested in the experiment, so I stayed and watched as the data streamed across the display screen.

My position in the University of Arkansas Medical School was in the Department of Pediatrics, which was located in Arkansas Children's Hospital. This was the largest department in the university with over 100 faculty members. I had an office in the Center for Applied Research and Education, a subdivision of the department. My dissertation work compared the brain activity of children with a reading disability to the brain activity of children with normal reading ability during certain reading and listening tasks.

When conducting the reading disability study I added a six-minute protocol that involved listening to my six primary sounds. The children participating in my study listened to these sounds before the main study. The primary sounds came at five-second intervals, and one sound was repeated six times before another sound was introduced. That gave me thirty seconds of a person listening to a single sound. Each sound was presented for two thirty-second intervals.

I wanted to see how the sounds might evoke different physiological responses. From the EKG data, I thought we might find an increased heart rate for the arousing "*rrr*" sound and a decrease in heart rate for the "*aah*." From the EEG data I thought that the "*sss*" sound of internal control might be connected to more frontal activity and the *"eee"* with less frontal activity since executive functioning, or thinking that involves controlling your environment, has been shown to be associated with the brain's frontal lobes. Finally, I thought that data from the GSR might show a larger-than-normal anxiety response to the *"ooh"* sound and a smaller one to the *"mmm"* sound.

After the last of my thirty-two students finished the study I began the data analysis. With a collection rate of 256 data points per each connection per second and 18 data collection sites, 16 EEG, EKG, and GSR, and six minutes of data on sounds for each child, I gathered over forty-seven million bits of information—a mind-boggling number that required sophisticated programs to both capture and analyze.

I sat in my office on a Friday morning pondering the methodology of the experiment. I had written the stimulus presentation program in a computer language called "C." I also helped to write the data collection program written in "C" and a more cryptic programming language called Assembly Language. My FORTRAN program reduced the data into a format utilized by my BMDP, or Bio-Medical Data Program, the statistical analysis program and final step in the process. I had developed proficiency in all these computer programming languages since launching my research career. With each new language I felt more and more like a computer geek and less and less like the spiritual seeker who had arrived in academia a few years earlier.

I felt a bit wistful thinking about my transition into the role of scientist as I finalized the BMDP program, ran it, and sent the output to the printer that morning. On the way to pick up the results I noticed the time—almost noon. I grabbed the printout and headed out the door.

Most every Friday I stopped by Meryl's work and took her out for lunch. She worked in the Infant Health and Development division of Arkansas Children's Hospital just a short distance from my lab. Her teaching background and work with child care had landed her a position working to enhance the cognitive development of infants at risk for learning disabilities.

That morning we chose one of our favorite restaurants, a small, vegetarian, cafeteria-style place toward West Little Rock that operated on a "pay what you think it is worth" basis. After filling our plates and placing our "donation" in the basket amid the spoons, forks, and napkins on the center island, we found a seat in the section with cushions and low tables in the manner of a Japanese Tea House. After catching up on my wife's morning I took the folded printout from my shirt pocket, flattened it out next to me, and studied it.

"What's that?"

"Oh, I finished the analysis of my one study right before I left for lunch. I want to check out the results." I didn't look up from the paper in front of me as I spooned some squash soup into my mouth.

"Which study?"

"The one I did on sounds," I said. I continued to read the probability levels of all the ANOVAs, the statistical tests that I employed to ascertain whether different sounds generated different physiological responses in the children who participated in the study. When I finished I shook my head.

"What's wrong?"

"Oh, disappointing results."

"Really? Does that mean you have to start your dissertation work over?" Meryl voiced her concern about a possible roadblock to earning my Ph.D.

I shook my head. "No. The data from my dissertation project is fine. This project," I said, pointing to the paper, "has no connection to my dissertation." I had already seen very encouraging results from the Ph.D. study.

"That's good," Meryl said, relief evident in her tone.

I had told her about my study with sounds several weeks earlier, but her apparent failure to remember indicated to me she didn't have an interest. That didn't bother me, though. We shared much in our lives. Having separate interests allowed our individuality to come through. I didn't bore her with the details about how the results disappointed me.

The only hint of an interesting result came from the EKG responses to the "*rrr*" and "*aah*." The "*rrr*" sounds produced a higher heart rate in some subjects, and the "*aah*" a slower heart rate, but only for the first three times these sounds appeared. Once a sound was heard a couple of times subjects tuned it out and their physiological responses went back to the same values recorded before the sound started. Some subjects were able to block out the effect entirely. The main problem seemed akin to the issue with my study conducted with Tufts students. The children did not actively engage in processing the sounds. They just sat passively in the chair while sounds came over the speakers. Getting no interesting results from such a hastily thrown together experiment that didn't require subjects to process any information shouldn't have surprised me.

    I didn't give up hope on my theory of sounds and emotions, however. In the study run at Tufts the *"mmm"* rated most pleasant. There was a published study showing *"ooh"* as unpleasant, and the *"aah"* and *"rrr"* did almost evoke the appropriate relaxing/arousing results. The weakest link in my theory concerned the connection between *"sss"* and control and *"eee"* and lack of control, although I did have some anecdotal and converging evidence pointing to these associations. In my mind those relationships were clear, but I wanted to design a more sophisticated experiment and demonstrate them with strong, empirical evidence.

# Chapter 35

*October 1995, Little Rock, AR*

Living in Arkansas offered at least one advantage over the Boston area. The cost of housing was about one-third. However, there was a price to pay for this savings—a relative lack of intellectually stimulating cultural opportunities that suited my taste. One way I fought the isolation of a "Yankee" in the south was to attend programs offered at the Unitarian Universalist Church of Little Rock, including meetings of the local chapter of the Institute of Noetic Sciences, or IONS. When I met one of the leaders of the IONS group at a weekend camping trip sponsored by the Unitarian church and told her about my research on the use of sounds for emotional balance, she invited me to speak on the topic at an IONS meeting. Although my two experiments failed to corroborate my entire scheme of how speech sounds affect emotions, I managed to collect various bits and pieces of data from other work that filled holes left by my work. Altogether it made a solid theory and validated my personal experiences. I felt ready to present it to the world.

The Little Rock IONS group met on the first Thursday of every month. I arrived a half-hour early to set up an overhead projector, then sat to look over my notes. Just before the meeting was scheduled to begin, a middle aged, slightly overweight woman with short dark hair and dressed in dark slacks and a bright colored blouse came over and offered her hand in introduction.

After introductions she asked what I would be speaking about. "My work with speech sounds and emotions."

"You're a therapist?"

"No. A researcher. I'm on the faculty of the University of Arkansas's Medical School."

Sharon raised her eyebrows. "What area of medicine?"

"I'm not a medical doctor. I have a Ph.D. in psychology."

She lit up. "A psychologist? I'm a counselor, a therapist. I work with emotionally disturbed children."

She gave me details of where she worked and the names of the psychologists she worked with to see if I knew any of them.

I shook my head and admitted that I didn't know any of her colleagues. As she talked I fantasized how we might collaborate and apply my understanding of sounds and emotions in a therapeutic setting, a practical application. Was this person's early appearance a chance occurrence, or did it portend more?

After a brief business meeting the president introduced me. The group gave a polite round of applause as I walked to the front of the small room.

"I want to thank Joan for inviting me here tonight," I said. It was good to finally get a chance to speak on the topic that captured my heart and soul. A centering energy made me feel alive and focused.

For the next hour I presented my research. I spoke about primary vowel sounds and how our physiology transforms each vowel into a consonant through constriction of the airway. How the jaw, lowest for an "*aah*," rises to create an "*rrr*." How the lips, pursed open for an "*ooh*," close to an "*mmm*," and how the tongue rises from its position for an "*eee*" to sound an "*sss*."

I moved on to talk about the physiology of emotions and the three dimensions of emotions—arousal, pleasure, control—and how the different parts of the brain contributed to the formation of a new emotional dimension as the brain evolved. How the brain stem, evolved since early reptiles, controls arousal. How the limbic system, a mammalian brain feature, plays the biggest part in control of pleasure reactions, and how the cortex, the highest evolved part of the human brain, accounts for aspects of emotional control.

The final part of my talk involved putting the two sections together into one coherent structure, much like a beautiful crystal. How the sounds controlled primarily by the jaw modulate arousal. How the lips modulate pleasantness, and the tongue control.

At first I saw intense engagement in the look on Sharon's face and others, but by the time I finished with the scientific details, some in the audience were getting that glazed-over look. I knew I had to switch gears to keep from losing them altogether. I notched up the excitement in my voice.

"I want to spend the rest of my time going over some well-known mantras and breaking them down into what they are saying emotionally.

"Let's start with one of the Hindu words for God, 'Ram.' Some advocate this word as a mantra for daily use. It is the word that Ghandi spoke immediately after he was shot. This word works by taking an aroused state, articulated by the '*rrr,*' and relaxing via the '*aah*', which then allows you to feel good, as expressed by the '*mmm*'. You could apply this formula in everyday situations whenever you want to reduce your arousal level from a hyper-aroused, agitated state.

"Note that you would not use this mantra during meditation. Why? Because the word starts with an arousing '*rrr*' sound. Remember, the initial letter of a mantra should start with a sound that matches your mood. If you are in a relaxed, meditative state, then the word 'AUM', the word for God in Sanskrit in the yoga tradition, works. This word takes a relaxed '*aah*' and then moves the negative '*ooh*' into a pleasant '*mmm*'.

"Now let's turn to a word from the Islamic tradition," I told the group. "The word 'Majeed' is one of the names of Allah and said to represent the glorious attribute of Allah. It usually gets translated as the Most Glorious One."

As soon as I mentioned "names of Allah," Sharon stood and shot me a look of disgust. Then she walked briskly out of the room without looking back. I suppressed a feeling of panic. Had I done something wrong? Could the mention of the Islamic name for God offend someone that much?

I managed to continue with my analysis of "Majeed" and then presented a few more examples before my time ran out.

After the meeting I chatted with many who expressed appreciation and interest in my work. It felt good to share my ideas, even though not everyone had kept an open mind.

Later that night when I arrived at home Meryl greeted me.

"How'd it go?"

"Good, good."

"I bet everyone liked your presentation," she said and gave me a hug. Even though she never expressed interest in the details of my work with sounds, she always supported my efforts.

"You're sweet." I gave her a kiss. With all the things going on in her life—raising three adolescents, holding down a full-time job, and running a household—she didn't have time enough to get involved in details of my work, but I felt her unwavering, unquestioning, emotional support.

# CHAPTER 36

*October 1996, Rural Southern NH*

I cherished every opportunity to speak about sounds and emotions at informal settings, like the Noetic Sciences meeting, and more formal ones at conferences, where I had to leave my family behind sometimes for a week at a time and fly to another U.S. city. There I would speak to a national or international audience who also came from great distances to listen to a variety of experts in a particular field. One set of such presentations included the 1995 and 1996 International Sound Colloquiums.

The content of my 1995 talk closely paralleled the Little Rock Noetic Sciences presentation. Just as in Little Rock, when the first example of a name of Allah was mentioned, a participant left, but I took it more in stride this time. I wasn't going to let another person's prejudice influence my work.

In 1996, I went into the relationships of non-primary sounds to emotions. That lecture focused on the emotional essence of individual sounds. I covered all English and some non-English speech sounds. The main theme centered on the role of physiological processes in the production of non-primary sounds, and how the position of the jaw, lips, and tongue determines emotional content of even non-primary sounds.

The International Sound Colloquium meetings differed from the majority of scientific conferences I attended while on the medical school faculty, in that a majority of attendees had no association with academia. Most had jobs as therapists and had a keen interest in the use of sound in non-traditional, typically healing ways.

The conference took place at a remote venue most often used for spiritual retreats. The setting reminded me of Kripalu Ashram, only now instead of being a seeker, I was a teacher. Instead of my spirit soaring from chanting, it surged from disseminating knowledge.

Although well over 200 people attended from dozens of states and a couple of foreign countries—including Canada, Russia, and South Africa—the conference had a very intimate feel. Participants mingled and shared meals in a common area, and because of the remote location virtually all joined in these meals. At one evening meal, two people—Linda, a massage therapist from Georgia, and Tony, an artist from Maine—joined me for dinner.

"So where did you get those examples that you used today in your talk?" Linda asked.

"Different sources," I replied, "but the ones that hold the most power for me are those from the Islamic tradition. They are known as the ninety-nine names of Allah."

"Allah has ninety-nine names?" she asked. "Where did he get all of them?"

"I believe they appear in the Qur'an, the holy book of Islam," I said.

"Yes, they are used by the Sufis," Tony added.

"Oh, so we have another expert?" Linda gave Tony a teasing look. "How do you know that?"

I could tell from her flirtatious tone that these two had spent time together.

"I'm a member of the Sufi Order of the West," Tony replied.

Linda raised her eyebrows. Then she turned to me and asked, "Are you a Sufi, too?"

Part of me wanted to say, "Not in this lifetime," but I refrained. "No," I told her.

"Then how did you come to learn the names of Allah?" she asked.

"That's a long story," I said, pausing to gauge her interest.

"I'm not going anywhere soon," she smiled.

I returned her smile and settled into my story, starting with my vision of the three Sufis and how the book *Toward the One* somewhat magically landed in my hands shortly thereafter.

"About a year after the vision I came across a small volume called *Ninety-Nine Names of Allah*. I memorized them and in the process saw the names of Allah as more than just a random list. My studies led me to graduate school where I studied sound and emotions and got my Ph.D."

"So did they teach you the names in grad school?" Linda sounded incredulous.

"Oh, no. No," I laughed. "I studied them on my own."

"And while studying the names a light just went off?" Linda asked, trying to understand my learning process.

"Not exactly," I told her. "It was a slow process of understanding rather than a sudden inspirational leap."

I relayed my discovery of the importance of the initial sound in a word, how I learned to apply the names to match my mood by repeating them on the subway, at lunch, or in any place where I had to pass time or wanted a break.

"This process led to my final breakthrough," I said.

"How's that?"

"Well, because I did most of this self-study on public transportation in the Boston area, I would sub-vocalize the names. I figured that speaking the names of Allah out loud would generate too much negative attention and disapproval, maybe even get me beat up, who knows. By using sub-vocalizations I came to realize two related modes of expression in addition to speech that have a significant emotional impact."

"Sub-vocalizations and what else?" she asked, following intently.

"Sub-vocalization—moving the vocal tract without speaking—was one mode," I confirmed. "I think of that like breathing the words. You move the lips, tongue, and jaw, but not the vocal cords.

"After making this realization and confirming it over repeated trials, it struck me that I should also be able to benefit by simply thinking the names. But I couldn't just simply think of a word willy-nilly. I first picked the proper word for my current mood, and then experienced the feelings associated with subsequent letters, all the while keeping my vocal tract immobile.

"Once I developed this ability and let my mind flow through the emotions, this benefit topped both breathing and speaking the word."

"Really? You just have to think about the words?" Linda sounded incredulous.

"Yes, that's right," I asserted. "In fact, as the level of use gets more refined, the effect gets more powerful."

Tony now broke his silence. "That's right," he said with conviction, "because by the time you get to the highest level, you own that name."

Linda addressed Tony. "Teach me how you breathe or think a name. Give me a specific example."

Tony looked at me, as if waiting for me to answer. I remained silent. I had a great curiosity about how the Sufis taught these practices and wanted Tony to fill us in.

"Come on. I wanna know," Linda poked him flirtatiously.

"Well," Tony said with downcast eyes. "I kinda took an oath that I wouldn't discuss those things." Linda looked crestfallen as Tony shifted the conversation to upcoming events.

Yet Tony's initial response to my ideas on sub-vocalizing and thinking the names of Allah created a significant impact on me. Up until that point I'd explored these ideas mostly on my own. Pir Vilayat's *Toward the One*, had put my thinking into gear, but I applied the accelerator and steered the course under my own power. Now that a member of the Sufi order had confirmed some of my most important conclusions with obvious conviction, I felt validated. Had I uncovered the secrets of the Sufis? Those secrets that Tony had taken an oath to keep? Something inside of me now told me "Yes."

If twelve years ago I had joined the Sufi Order of the West, I might have learned those secrets with help instead of pushing through the difficult path alone. But then my lips would have been as silent as Tony's. I would not have experienced the joy of sharing my knowledge with others.

# CHAPTER 37

*March 1998, La Jolla, San Diego, CA*

"Can I help you?"

I looked up from the paper I'd been staring at—a layout of the La Jolla Hyatt conference center in the program guide for the *The International Psychology of Consciousness Energy Medicine and Dynamic Change* conference. I must have appeared lost as I stood in the intersection of two corridors.

"Oh? Thanks." I said with a smile to the short, plump, middle-aged woman who looked at me over the top of her wire-rim glasses. She wore a black dress, black pumps and no jewelry. Her somber look stood out among the other attendees of the conference. "Do you work here?"

She gave a small, self-conscious laugh. "No. I'm attending the conference. I live close by, so I guess I just feel more at home than most."

"Oh." I registered a paradoxical distant and welcoming look in her eyes. A bit perplexed I stammered, "Uh, well, I was just wondering which way to Delphi B?"

She gave a quick glance at the map. "It's down at the end of that hall," she said, and pointed off to my right. "You aren't going to a meeting there now, are you? It's lunchtime."

"No. Just getting oriented. I have to give a presentation there later this afternoon."

"Oh, what is your topic?"

I flipped the brochure back to the page for Friday afternoon presentations. "Here," I said, pointing to the entry that listed my talk on "Treating Depression, Anxiety, and Stress with Intentional Speech and Breath."

"That sounds interesting. I'll have to check it out."

"Good. Well, thanks for the orientation."

We both managed a small laugh. She then turned and started to walk away. After a moment's thought I took a few brisk steps and caught up. "Excuse me. Could you tell me of some good local choices for lunch? I didn't order one through the conference."

"Sure. I was just going out myself. Do you want to go with me?"

Beth drove us to a little outdoor café in Del Mar a few miles up the coast where we sat in the sun and ordered vegetarian fare. She asked about my presentation and I told her about my work. By the end of the meal I tired of talking about myself.

"What drew you to this conference?" I asked.

She told me about her stalled efforts in a clinical psychology Ph.D. program. She had started the program five years ago, at forty years of age, the same age I was when I started my graduate studies.

"But I haven't done anything toward finishing in over a year. I just can't seem to get back on track."

"Why not?" I asked.

There was a long pause as she twisted her napkin. Finally, without looking up, she spoke in a slow, soft voice. "I lost my husband fifteen months ago."

"I'm sorry to hear that."

After another long break she continued.

"Heart attack. He was only forty-eight."

More silence before she spoke.

"He was an M.D. We were going to go into practice together."

After several more seconds she looked up and forced a smile. "My friends tell me 'It's been fifteen months. Snap out of it,' but it's not that easy."

I could see tears welling in her eyes. I wanted to say "I understand" to reassure her, but I was sure that I didn't understand, so I remained silent.

After a big exhale, she said, "I have just been staying at home, missing him, so finally today I told myself I would go to this conference and make a point of meeting someone." This time the smile seemed less forced.

"Well, I'm glad to have met you and have you as my tour guide."

"Have you been to San Diego before?" she asked, her tone turning positive.

"I attended a conference in Mission Bay a few years ago, but I hadn't explored this far north."

She looked at her watch. "It's a little after one o'clock. Do you have to get back to the conference?"

I shook my head. "I wasn't planning on attending any sessions before mine at four o'clock."

So we drove north along the coast a few miles, past the Self-Realization Fellowship ashram, before turning inland. After meandering through several expensive neighborhoods we turned into a cul-de-sac where she stopped the car.

"This is where I used to live." She pointed to one of the houses almost hidden by landscaping.

"I haven't been back here since my husband died. He died in that house and I had to leave. I got a realtor to list it and sell it without my stepping foot in it again. I paid movers to pack up and move all of my stuff."

The emotion was palpable in her voice.

"It must be hard for you to do this."

"I didn't ever think I could come back here." She took a deep breath and slowly exhaled. "Thanks for coming with me. I don't think I could have come here alone."

We sat in silence for about a minute before she started the car. We drove back to the coast without conversation and stopped at a small public beach. She took off her shoes and we walked along the sandy shoreline. When we reached the end of the public area and turned to start back she looked at me.

"Do you believe it's possible to contact my husband? I mean, do you think that I should pay a medium to try to contact him?"

I managed an evasive, "I don't know."

This was before John Edward popularized the concept of contacting the dead, but the questions shouldn't have surprised me. This was California, and over fifteen years earlier a California psychic told me I was going to become a medium. As my uncle from Palo Alto once told me, "Everything seems to happen in California first, before spreading to the rest of the country."

Her sincerity and hopefulness disarmed me. My non-committal, almost dismissive reply made me feel uncomfortable. I felt like I was trying to avoid telling the truth. I had never spoken to anyone about my astral travel and reincarnation experiences, but looking at a woman with a broken heart changed that.

"I do believe that it is possible for existence outside of the physical body," I finally said.

As we walked to the car and then drove back to the conference center I told her how I'd learned about astral travel and what I believed about my own reincarnation. As I described these events it seemed as though someone else did the talking. I had kept these things private for so long that I found it hard to believe it was me speaking. Who was this person?

The part of me that worked so hard to succeed in academia wanted to deny my past. The majority of academics see paranormal events as myths, and they ostracize anyone who purports belief in them. By giving hope to this grieving woman in her quest to contact her dead mate, was I spreading false hope? I knew many who would say that was so, but I couldn't deny the part in me that believed the death of the body was not the final act of the person. That part of me won.

This conversation revitalized the seeker in me and increased my desire to reconcile the human race's ability to travel in an astral body with the science of evolution. If I felt compelled to talk about astral travel, I wanted the intellectual ability to defend the concept.

# Chapter 38

*July 1999, Memphis, TN*

The central disillusionment with my faculty position stemmed from having to spend over ninety percent of my time in research funded by government grants in which I could muster only marginal interest. The lab director expected me to continue the lines of research already funded. I had specific working orders not to branch off in a direction in which no prior work existed because agencies would not fund such endeavors. With no opportunity to pursue my own research I felt trapped. The San Diego trip brought into focus my need to make a change. To stay meant stagnation.

Starting in 1996, I looked for positions at smaller colleges and universities where I would be able to continue my own research, but I never landed a spot. I ruled out geographical areas more than a short drive from our families' homes in Pennsylvania, due to Meryl's wishes, and in two years I only applied to two positions, never getting past the first interviews.

I decided to take another track and leave academia. I still held a desire to complete further research on sounds and emotions, but I harbored a stronger need for change. Another chance in academia would have to wait.

As the Dot-Com era fueled a tremendous growth in high paying tech jobs, in the fall of 1998 I posted my resume on the web. With the wealth of programming and database experience that came from running a highly technical lab, I got a call from a recruiter the next day. Our conversation was followed by an introductory phone interview two days later, a follow-up phone interview the next week, and a job offer the day after that.

I took a position as consultant with a large software company. I flew all over the country and to Canada and Europe to do consulting work and training for a newly developed software product. It wasn't research on sounds and emotions, but it was exciting and paid well. In just over a year's time I accumulated enough frequent flyer points to earn Gold status with three different airlines. I got plenty of first-class upgrades and earlier flights though standby.

One summer day I finished teaching a training class early on Friday morning. After a long week of classes I was ready to get back home. I caught the 2:10 flight out of Detroit to Memphis and hoped to get the 5:20 to Little Rock instead of waiting for the 7:55.

"Could you put me on standby?" I asked the attendant at the Northwest Airlines counter.

"I can," came the polite reply as she took my ticket and typed into the terminal in front of her.

"How far down on the list am I?" I asked.

"You're third," replied the attendant.

"What are my chances?" I asked.

"We're overbooked," she said without looking up.

I felt deflated. All that rush just to sit in the Memphis airport. "Well, hopefully my flight won't get canceled this time," I mumbled as I walked away from the counter. The previous week I had been slated for the last flight from Memphis to Little Rock but the plane had mechanical problems. The airline put me up in an airport hotel where I got to feel, not to mention hear, FedEx planes take off every two minutes as the room shook and car alarms right outside my window went off from the jets' vibrations.

Resigned to waiting, I found a seat near an outlet and plugged in my laptop to start building a training program for another new software product.

A woman's voice came on the overhead speakers in the waiting area. "We need two volunteers to give up their seats in exchange for a voucher for a free flight." The noise blended in with the many other boarding announcements so I hardly noticed. A few minutes later the same voice said, "We still need one more volunteer to give up their seat for a free flight."

After several more minutes the attendants started boarding passengers.

"They must have finally got someone to give up their seat," an older gentleman remarked to his companion as they rose to get in line.

The seats around me emptied, but I hardly noticed as I kept working. Several minutes after the announcement for all rows to board I was startled by my name coming across the speakers.

I folded my laptop, put it in its case, and walked up to the counter. "Yes, you called my name?"

"Can I have your boarding pass?" she asked.

I handed her my ticket, wondering why she wanted it.

She scanned my pass and then handed it back to me. "You can board now."

I didn't ask for an explanation, but hurried down the jetway. I entered the door of the DC-9 and started down the aisle, trying to piece together what had happened. They must not have been able to get a single person to volunteer to give up the last seat. So they settled for a couple, which meant an empty seat. Then the two people in front of me on the standby list must have been together. I figured it out as I reached the back of the plane and the only empty seat.

I sat down beside a thin, attractive, middle-aged woman with bronze-colored skin.

"Wow!" I exclaimed, unable to contain my feeling of good fortune. "I can't believe I made it on this flight."

"Yes, they were asking people to give up their seats just a few minutes ago," she said.

"My lucky day." Since her tone was engaging I continued, "Are you from the Little Rock area or just going to visit?"

"I live in Pine Bluff."

I was familiar with the area, an hour south of Little Rock. "Are you from there originally?" I was almost certain that this was wrong. Her features were Middle Eastern and Pine Bluff was not known as an international city.

"Oh, no. I'm from Egypt. I moved here to work at the University of Arkansas at Pine Bluff."

"Oh, I used to work for the University of Arkansas Medical School in the Department of Pediatrics."

"Do you know Dr. Phillips?"

"Yes, he's the director of the Center for Applied Research where I worked."

"I work with him on the USDA nutrition project," she said with a broad smile. "My name is Makara." She held out her hand and I shook it as I introduced myself.

"I worked on the USDA nutrition project, too." I smiled, feeling a little nostalgia for the project I left nine months earlier. "I studied infants with a Failure to Thrive diagnosis in the electrophysiology lab," I said. "What's your role?"

"I'm a nutritionist. I work with low-income parents in raising awareness of nutrition needs."

"Oh." I nodded. My mind was having a hard time grasping the serendipity of the situation. Then my mind went back to her nationality. "Your native language is Arabic, right?"

"Yes, is my accent showing that much?"

"Oh, I didn't mean it that way. I have studied some Arabic words and wasn't sure how to pronounce them. Perhaps you could help me."

"No problem. What words?"

Fate has strange ways of working. I might have given up my research position, but somehow an opportunity for practical research on the names of Allah just appeared in the seat next to mine.

"Do you know the ninety-nine names of Allah?"

Makara grimaced. "I'm not sure I remember them all. It has been a while since I have recited them." She recalled the practice of daily recitation of the names. "How did you learn them? Are you a Muslim?"

"No, I was inspired by a book written by a Sufi. I learned a written English translation of the names and only heard a few of them spoken. I'd like to hear how they should really sound."

"I would be glad to help, if I can remember them."

"I know how they are written in English."

I reached into the flap of my laptop bag and pulled out a notebook and pen. As I wrote down each name of Allah, she pronounced it for me and I repeated it back, sometimes two or three times to make sure I said it correctly. We spent a half-hour going over all of the names. *The Ninety-Nine Names of Allah* used an easy-to-follow, phonetic spelling. Thus, my prior pronunciation for a majority of the names proved accurate. However, certain Arabic letters have no direct English translation. Names which contained those letters always stymied me in my earlier efforts. With Makara's help, I said those names correctly for the first time—or at least close to the proper way, given my lack of experience with Arabic.

When we finished, Makara asked, "Why do you want to learn how to say the names of Allah?"

It didn't strike me until that point that it would be unusual for a non-Muslim to study the names of Allah. "I am interested in how the sounds in each name go together, to evoke a specific emotional state that can bring emotional stability and harmony to a person."

Makara looked puzzled. "How did you reach such a conclusion?"

I chuckled and launched into a mini-version of one of my talks on sounds and emotions. When it became apparent that I was finished speaking, Makara said, "So, you believe the emotional impact of the names of Allah can be rationally explained and understood?"

"I believe each name has a unique emotional impact that makes it appropriate for a particular situation. In fact, I use the names as personal mantras or prayers to maintain emotional stability."

She again looked surprised. "Can you give me an example of how you use them?"

"Take the name 'Haadee'," I said.

"Yes, it means 'The Guide'."

"Well, in my current job I often conduct training sessions, and this name helps me better get my points across when I am having difficulty. I chose that word, not based on its translation, but because of the sequence of sounds. It is easy to train people when everyone gets it, but whenever it is difficult to get something across, I find myself getting frustrated. For the name to work as a way to deal with a problem, the initial sound of the name must match your mood. The name then takes you from that mood along a path toward a different mood expressed by the rest of the name. If the initial sound of the name doesn't match your mood, then the name is disconnected from your current emotional state. The '*h*' sound corresponds to frustration."

I let out an exasperated sounding "*h*."

"Then how I want to deal with the frustration dictates what sound should follow the '*h*'. In a situation where I am teaching, frustration can keep me from being effective. In order to overcome the frustration I need to relax, which is the '*aah*' sound. Then once I am relaxed, I need to focus on the knowledge I am trying to deliver. The '*d*' sound helps me to achieve that focus. So in the name 'Haadee' the '*d*' sound achieves the control I need. Once I have the focus, I simply need to let the situation unfold without any further tampering. I can get there through the '*ee*' sound."

Makara look satisfied by my explanation. "I'm not sure that I understand it all, but I am fascinated."

The flight attendant announced our approach into Little Rock. During the last few minutes of the flight I gave her a detailed explanation of the emotional impact of another name.

After I concluded Makara looked excited. "Have you analyzed all ninety-nine in that manner?" she asked.

"Most, but not all," I told her.

"Maybe if I gave you my email address you could send me more information?" Makara pulled out a business card and handed it to me. I handed her one of my cards. Then she continued, "I wonder whether you would be interested in talking at my mosque? Many of our members are from the University and I think they would find your material very interesting."

The thought intrigued me, but there was a problem. "We just sold our house in Little Rock and are moving back to Pennsylvania. And after we move..." My voice trailed off and I shrugged.

Makara looked disappointed but said, "I understand."

"But I'll be sure to email you the additional information," I promised.

The ground came closer and closer and the plane finally touched down. A good day had become even better because I got to speak with somebody who spoke Arabic. I had that familiar high that I often caught from working with sounds. As I got into a waiting cab, one thought brought me down. *Too bad I can't take her up on her offer.*

# Chapter 39

*September 1999, Pine Bluff, AR*

Moving my family back to Pennsylvania proved emotionally difficult. My son held a job with a computer retailer and was in a serious relationship, so he moved into his own apartment. It was hard to see him stay behind in Arkansas, but we felt satisfied that he would do fine on his own.

My two daughters were both in high school. They protested even more than they had when we left Boston. It was a difficult decision to take them away from their friends again, especially at this critical point in their social lives. However, Meryl and I felt the need to be closer to both sets of our parents, whose health was failing.

Meryl and I always found a way to agree on family matters, but when it came to intellectual matters, finding common ground proved more difficult. After leaving academia I pursued the use of sounds on my own, learning and writing more as I did, but I chose not to speak with Meryl on the topic. I'd given up trying to bounce ideas off of her about sounds and emotions. She never saw my point of view. We always went back to our familiar mode of academic rivalry. I wondered whether her reluctance to accept any of my conclusions stemmed from the work's origin. When I first became fascinated with the use of sounds and mantras, we were struggling economically. Perhaps Meryl wanted me to let go of ideas she associated with a less prosperous time.

Undeniably, though, I felt a strong urge to share my research with others. After my family settled back in Pennsylvania I emailed Makara and set up a time to speak at her mosque. Then early one Friday afternoon I flew to Little Rock, rented a car, and drove to the Ramada Inn in Pine Bluff where Makara picked me up.

On the trip to the mosque with Makara I felt excited, and because of Makara's reticent mood, a bit nervous, but the atmosphere at the mosque allayed my apprehensions. Dr. Ramejaddin's friendly manner, the imam's sonorous voice, and the reverent attitudes of the faithful all soothed me. The tension from the morning of work, the hectic trip to the airport, the line at the car rental counter, and the hour drive to Pine Bluff melted away as I listened to the prayers fill the hall.

I began my talk with no idea where my words would lead me. The choice to speak about my vision came without premeditation. I wasn't talking to academics, but to a group of religious believers. My work with the names of Allah traced back to the vision, so there I began.

When the man shoved his way through the women and demanded, "Why are you listening to this infidel?" I stared at him in disbelief.

After a long moment of silence one of the seated men told him, "Sit down and be quiet."

"No," the new arrival protested. "This is a disgrace!"

"What is your problem?" another asked the loud man.

"Yes, you should sit down and listen," said another. "We want to hear what he has to say."

"Who are you?" one in the congregation asked the intruder.

"I am from Little Rock," he answered. "When I heard that a Christian was speaking here tonight I felt that somebody had to put a stop to it."

"Why do you think we should not listen to a Christian?" another asked the new arrival.

"The Qur'an says we should defend Islam from infidels. Why are you not standing with me?"

"The prophet, peace be unto him, said that we can learn from non-believers. This person came here from out of state on his own time and money to talk to us about what his scientific studies show about Islam. Let him speak," Dr. Ramejaddin spoke this time.

"Yes, we want to hear what he has to say," a man repeated.

The statement about the prophet seemed to mollify the angry man, at least for the moment, so he sat down. When it appeared that he didn't have a retort to the prophet's advice, or at least did not want to appear to be going against the prophet, I resumed my talk. But I only got in two more sentences before he interrupted again. "This person is not one of us. We should not be listening to him," he urged the others.

Finally, I had heard enough. I felt the support of the others and couldn't hold back my growing anger.

"If you would just listen, you would see that what I am saying is very supportive of Islam," I said with a definite edge to my voice. I learned during my roaming days that if a dog attacked you, you never retreated. That only encouraged the animal to pursue a frightened prey.

"Yes, just be quiet."

"Be quiet."

Two others backed me up. The man sat with a sullen look, but said nothing more during the talk.

I gave a brief explanation on the basic associations between emotions and components of speech. After I had completed this broad outline I launched into a discussion of how this information concerning the connections between speech and emotions can be applied to the names of Allah.

"The names of Allah can be useful in many ways. Some allow you to better help others, some work to help yourself overcome personal problems. For an example of helping others there is the name 'Kareem', translated as 'The Generous One'. This name can be used whenever you have resources that you want to put to work."

I explained the '*k*' sound represents an active control of a situation. The short '*a*' moves you to the next consonant, '*rrr*', indicates putting energy into something. The '*eee*' denotes surrender to the situation, allowing your energy to be utilized as Allah would see fit. The last sound, the '*mmm*', is the emotional reward, the pleasant feeling you get when you have done something to help others.

I paused to see if anyone had a question. When nobody spoke, I gave several more examples and answered questions, all voiced with an attitude of wanting to understand and none filled with disdain or derision. Afterwards they served refreshments and I got a chance to speak with some of the men as we ate.

"I enjoyed your talk very much," one man told me as we ate pizza that had been set out on a tablecloth on the floor. "You have come a long way to be here?"

"I live in Pennsylvania," I said. "My work takes me all over the United States. I usually go home on the weekends, but I chose to come here to talk to you instead."

"This must be very important to you for you to do that," he commented.

I nodded, but didn't say anything.

After a few moments he said, "Why don't you become a Muslim?" My status as a non-Muslim had been assumed, although I never formally claimed as much. My simple lack of declaration of the faith and non-participation in the prayer service was proof enough, I supposed.

"I have thought about that," I confessed, "but it would be hard for my family. Also, I think that my work on the names of Allah may be more widely accepted if it is seen as coming from a non-Muslim." I didn't tell him the most important reason—that to me the names of Allah had emotional significance due to their inherent nature, rather than a religious belief.

After the event I walked back to the car with Makara.

"You were very smart to start your talk with the story of your vision," Makara told me once we were in the car. "Most Muslims place importance on such happenings, more so than a typical Westerner."

I didn't reply. In fact, on the trip back to the hotel I didn't say much at all. I was feeling calm and relaxed after my excursion into a world I had never chanced before. At the hotel Makara got out of the car and we talked for a moment in the dark, hot Arkansas night under the light of the parking lot.

"Thank you so much for doing this," she told me.

"It was my pleasure," I assured her.

"You must keep in touch and email anything further that you have in your work on the names of Allah. Thanks again," she said as she held out her hand.

I didn't take her hand, but instead held open my arms. "Give me a hug," I said to her. She hesitated momentarily, her culture's taboo on contact between men and women evident. I continued, "You are like a sister to me."

She accepted my hug, and we said goodbye.

# CHAPTER 40

*July 2000, Carlisle, PA*

The idea of being a well-paid consultant who flies around the world and puts all expenses on a corporate credit card may sound appealing. However, the reality of the job loses its luster quickly. The isolation from family takes the biggest toll. When you are not there to help your wife deal with teenaged kids and academic or discipline troubles arising from school, it makes for rough weekends. After two years as part of the jet set and living on the road, I began to search for a less hectic lifestyle, one that would help shore up my family. Since I still had a desire to further my research on sounds and emotions, I decided to again try to get a position in academia.

Tenure track jobs were not plentiful. If you wanted to obtain one of these you had to be willing to go where the job was, not to mention fend off dozens of other applicants. I did not want to move again. My father and my wife's mother were not in good health, and our children did not want to be uprooted another time. So instead of tenure track I opted for a temporary position, a visiting professor, as it is euphemistically called.

I took a one-year stint at Dickinson College, a highly rated liberal arts college about a half-hour from our home. There I taught both Introduction to Cognitive Psychology and Experimental Cognitive Psychology, a three-hour laboratory class that met once a week.

In that course I designed an experiment that I hoped would provide evidence to support my theory of how speech sounds influence emotions. The experiment followed the design of a lexical decision task with priming. In simple terms, it required a "yes" or "no," in this case, in response to a group of letters. If the letters spelled a word, the response should be "yes." If the letters did not form a word, then the proper response would be "no." In order to get useful data the letters were presented on a screen for only a brief period, and subjects (the name given to participants in the experiment) were told to respond as quickly as possible or "as soon as they know."

A lexical decision task with priming involves exposing the person making the decision to another stimulus, called the prime, just prior to or simultaneous with the letters. The priming stimulus is designed to have different effects on different types or categories of words. That is, primes should make the lexical decision for some words easier, but not for others. For example, a prime of the word "doctor" will aid in the recognition of the target word "nurse," but a prime of the word "tree" will not help someone recognize "nurse." The priming effect reveals itself in faster "yes" responses and fewer incorrect "no" responses.

In this study I used speech sounds, or phonemes, such as "*rrr*" and "*mmm*" as the priming stimuli. The purpose of the study was to test whether certain speech sounds work as primes for targets that fell into certain emotional categories. For example, when a subject hears the sound "*mmm*," could he or she identify words associated with pleasure, like "gift," more easily than when they hear another sound, say "*rrr*"? Or when they hear the sound "*aah*," could they identify words associated with relaxation, like "massage," easier than when they hear another sound?

The nitty-gritty of most cognitive experiments is the selection of stimuli. It's important to get the stimuli right to eliminate possible confounds in the experiment's design. For this study I needed a list of twenty words that people would associate with each of the six emotional qualities: arousal, relaxation, pleasure, unpleasantness, control, and lack of control. For arousal, I used words like "fight" and "anger"; for relaxation, words like "snooze" and "massage"; for pleasantness words like "treat" or "enjoy"; for unpleasantness, words like "vomit" and "spider"; for feeling in control, words like "teacher" or "referee"; and for feeling out of control, words like "lunatic" or "scared." Getting the right twenty words for each of the emotion categories was crucial to the success of the experiment. I assigned each student one emotion dimension and required them to compose a list of at least forty words that they thought could potentially fit the two emotional extremes of their dimension. This gave us 240 words in all.

Next the students tested the potential words, using volunteers from my Introduction to Cognitive Psychology class, where students were required to volunteer for an experiment or write a paper. The volunteers rated each of the 240 potential words on each of the three dimensions of emotions: unpleasant to pleasant, relaxing to arousing, and out of control to in control.

After compiling their ratings, my students created six lists of twenty target words each. For each emotional category they picked the words rated highest for that attribute, but with one twist. I stipulated that each list of twenty emotional words needed to be balanced on word length and word frequency of usage. Once the students completed the list of emotional target words they added filler words and non-words to finalize the list of all targets.

The next step involved recording the priming sounds. After they overcame the technical phobias, they found this job easy and fun. By the time the students put the recorded primes and list of targets into the stimulus presentation program they were enthusiastic about the experiment.

My students all did an excellent job of creating stimuli and testing the subjects, more volunteers from my Intro class. By the end of the semester my third experimental effort to tie specific sounds to particular emotions had the convincing data I wanted.

My earlier attempts—of having Tufts students rate sounds, and taking physiological readings at Arkansas Children's Hospital while children listened to sounds—had fallen short because these protocols lacked the proper sophistication. The task of rating sounds was too vague and allowed too much subjectivity. Simple listening failed because subjects had not engaged with any stimuli and all of the physiological responses habituated.

I hit pay dirt with the lexical decision with priming task. The data analyses supported the hypotheses of my theory. Faster reaction times and significantly fewer errors occurred whenever the emotional target word had the proper priming sound. I found such priming effects, not for just one or two of the emotion-prime categories, but all six.

My contract to teach at Dickinson expired less than a month after the conclusion of the experiment, and I never got a chance to publish the results in a scholarly journal. However, I did get the satisfaction of finally generating solid evidence to support my theory about sounds and emotions.

# Chapter 41

*August 2001, Rural Columbia County, PA*

The warmth of the afternoon summer sun felt good after my dip into the spring-fed pond. I lay on the grass soaking up the heat and watching the clouds drift by like tufts of cotton floating upon an ocean of blue sky. The pond was the same as always, but the fields at SKY Land looked different than the last time I visited, eight years earlier. Where I once pitched my tent for a weekend, now a bull, a cow, and a calf wandered in their pasture letting out occasional bellows. A horse roamed what used to be an empty field just beyond that, and three dogs greeted every new arrival with a chorus of barks. No longer the tranquil retreat I knew in the past, SKY Land now resembled a real farm.

*I wish Meryl could have come along.* I mused about our past trips to the farm. She hadn't visited the place since we had come together almost twenty years earlier, but she opted out of the chance to return this time, as in all times since, in order to keep things running smoothly back home. I knew as a country-born girl she would have appreciated the rustic farm atmosphere, not to mention the chance to enjoy Indian food, her favorite ethnic cuisine.

A splashing noise interrupted my reverie as a young, athletic woman emerged from the water and sat down on the grass beside me. "The volleyball game was a lot of fun," Heather said as she shook water from her hair and rubbed her head with a towel.

"Volleyball is always a highlight of the weekend retreats," I said, without moving from my relaxed position. Every SKY Land program I ever attended included a volleyball game following the afternoon yoga class. That much of SKY Land hadn't changed.

Heather wrapped the towel around her head and leaned her slender body back on her elbows. "What a gorgeous day."

I didn't say anything, but kept smiling as my body soaked in warmth from the sun.

After a minute, she turned onto one elbow and said to me, "I read the four chapters you gave me last night. I really found them fascinating."

I got up on one elbow facing her. "Already?" I said, surprised. Heather was one of the featured practitioners at the retreat. She was a psychologist on the faculty of Thomas Jefferson Medical School and had conducted a guided meditation event in the Asana Hall the prior evening. After the session I gave her a copy of the first chapters of my work in progress. I called it *Holistic Emotive Practices*. It was my first attempt to put together all of my research into the connections between sounds and emotions and how these principles might be used to achieve emotional balance. I brought along a copy to the weekend retreat in hope of sharing it with someone and getting feedback. In fact, the opportunity to share my work with people who might "get it" provided my main motivation for coming to SKY Land.

"Yes. You present some great evidence and make interesting conclusions based on sound arguments. What university did you say you are with?" she asked.

"I'm no longer with a university. I did research at the University of Arkansas Medical School. Last year I was a visiting professor at Dickinson College. I was able to accomplish some interesting research there, but I guess I'm freelancing right now. I would like to get my work published eventually. This is my first effort at putting everything together into chapters for a book."

"Well, good luck. I know how hard it is to get published even when you're associated with a University. I imagine it will be a lot harder if you are on your own. Are you going to try to get back into academia?"

"I don't know. Perhaps. I left on my own accord because I wasn't satisfied..." my voice trailed off.

No doubt Heather could detect the uncertainty in my voice. Her instinct to counsel took over. "I'm surprised to hear you say that. You accomplished some interesting research."

"Yes, I think I did."

"Give me an example that really stands out to you."

I explained the experiment conducted by the students in my cognitive psychology lab course. It was easy to describe to a fellow psychologist in only a few sentences.

"And you say that you got statistically significant results?" she asked.

"A 'p' less than 0.02," I told her. That was statistical jargon psychologists use to indicate the probability of an event. In this instance it meant that the probability of the priming effect in my experiment happening by random chance was less than two chances in a hundred. A "p" less than 0.05, or five chances in a hundred, was considered "significant" or noteworthy.

"That's convincing," she said. "So why aren't you fighting to get back at it?"

I gave a sigh, looked away from her, and lay back down. "I guess it's my karma to take my trip outside of academia for now," I told her. "I have to go on with my life and make a living and support my family."

"What *are* you doing now?" she asked, still propped on her arm looking at me.

"I'm working as a database administrator for a hospital."

"Well, you're still in healthcare."

What might have been an attempt at consolation fell way short. "Yes, but not in research," I said flatly. I took a long deep breath and exhaled slowly, trying to overcome my deflated feeling. I tried to put a positive spin on my situation. "I'm using my technical skills and, to some extent, my people skills. I interact with lots of departments and create computer interfaces that make their jobs easier. I find it rewarding." After a brief pause, I added, "It pays the bills."

Heather lay down with her back on the grass and put her hands behind her head, just staring at the sky for over a minute. "Well, I am interested in what you've written. When you complete some more chapters be sure to send me a copy."

At last I felt some consolation. "Yes, I will. I would really like your feedback once I get into the details of the practices. Those first four chapters that I gave you are just the framework. I've been working on how to put mantras together and specific uses for them."

"Sounds good."

Although I had yearned for another academic position, it dawned on me that maybe academia wasn't ready for my work. Networking outside of a traditional university setting I was finding open-minded people interested in what I had to say. It gave me hope.

# CHAPTER 42

*September 2001, Chambersburg, PA*

In writing *Holistic Emotive Practices* I struggled with how to explain to readers that the example words came almost exclusively from Islam. My uncertainty was a result of the two times someone left a talk the moment I mentioned Islam. Their looks of disgust had told me they didn't like what they heard.

Although the Sufis and the names of Allah had a strong influence on the development of my ideas about sounds and emotions, I looked at plenty of other potential therapeutic words and mantras from other religions to include, especially from Hinduism, the richest tradition for religious names and mantras. But none of those other names or mantras seemed to offer the therapeutic benefit that fit into the framework of *Holistic Emotive Practices*. I needed short words that allow one to easily follow the emotional values of the sounds. The length of most Hindu and Sanskrit mantras makes tracking the feelings difficult, if not impossible.

That is not to say I didn't find these other mantras or words powerful. Indeed, many Hindu chants seemed quite potent. I certainly felt their energy on my visit to Kripalu twenty years earlier. But Hindu mantras seemed to function as a way to transport you to an altered state of consciousness, rather than solving or working through an emotional problem or concern. There is nothing inherently wrong in using a mantra to achieve an altered state, which fits with the goal of yoga of achieving union with God. The goal in *Holistic Emotive Processes*, however, focuses on applying sound–emotion relationships to solve real-life problems.

Because of the abrupt exits from my talks, I had avoided giving Heather completed chapters that included names of Allah, but after getting positive feedback from her that afternoon, I overcame my hesitancy. I emailed her several more chapters, ones which included examples using the Islamic names. She responded with encouragement and put me in touch with a Rabbi friend who had written a book on the use of sound in the Jewish tradition. This correspondence melted away much of my fear of rejection for using the names of Allah.

I got further momentum in getting my book published through a bit of serendipity at work. It came while I upgraded the physician credentialing system in the hospital. I saw a term on a printout and off-handedly identified it to Sherri, an administrator who used the system.

"*Ataxia telangiectasia.* That's a mouthful," I said, pointing to the words. "An inherited neurodegenerative disease that affects the cerebellum. Symptoms include sensitivity to x-rays."

"Where did you come up with that?" Sherri asked.

"Oh, I had to memorize all sorts of neurological disorders when I took the neuroanatomy course at the Med School."

"Yeah, right."

"What? You don't believe me?" I looked at her and laughed.

"You're kidding, aren't you?"

"No. I have a Ph.D. in psychology. I took a neuroanatomy course at a Med School in getting my degree."

"Really?" she said, unable to withhold her incredulity. "Why are you working in Information Services at a hospital?"

I found it painful to discuss, or even think about, life away from research. "I needed a job that pays money."

She didn't reply, apparently realizing that she had hit a sore spot. I noted her abrupt silence and continued, "I *am* writing a book on the research I have done."

Sherri immediately perked up. "Really? What's it on?"

"Sounds and emotions," I said, not taking my eyes off my work. I didn't want to get into details. The data transformation process of the credentialing system required all of my concentration.

"You should talk to my father," she said. "He's retired now, but he spent over thirty years in the publishing industry in New York City."

She set up a dinner meeting for me with her father. He offered encouragement, but also emphasized that getting published is challenging and takes persistence. He suggested ways to pitch the work and named publishers that might be most receptive. I felt ready to pursue my dream of publishing my work.

# Chapter 43

*September 11, 2001, Chambersburg, PA*

They say every American remembers exactly what they were doing when they first learned about it. I was sitting in my cubicle working on the Clinical Data Repository when I heard a loud exclamation from Karl in the cubicle across the aisle.

"That ain't right."

There were elements of pain and disbelief in his voice.

I could see he was staring at his computer monitor. I walked over to his desk to see a 747 impaled in one of the World Trade Center towers. That image, and those that followed—the plane hitting the second tower, the buildings collapsing—put me in a shocked state of disbelief. It brought back memories of seeing the tops of the twin towers years before as I flew in a little commuter prop plane circling Manhattan for landing at LaGuardia. They seemed so grand and magnificent, so commanding, and now they were gone. A feeling of innocence and virtue disappeared with them.

The event had a major impact on me personally. I'm not talking about the nightmares. Fortunately those lasted less than a month. The more lasting effect on my psyche involved my work on *Holistic Emotive Practices*.

I didn't agree with the wave of anti-Islamic fervor in the United States, but I could not escape the cognitive dissonance caused by my association with the names of Allah and the association of a band of worshipers of Allah with terrorism. I withdrew from my work on sounds and emotions.

In some ways I reverted to behavior of my early adulthood—walking in the woods and fields of central Pennsylvania. I didn't quit my job this time though. I had responsibilities including one daughter in college, and another one set to go the next year. So my walking, or I should say hiking since my excursions always involved a pack, was after work and on weekends.

# CHAPTER 44

*July 2006, The Tuscarora Trail, Central PA*

Hiking did more than help me forget about my struggle with the Islamic connection to my work. It fulfilled something in me, something I had been missing. When I started to hike in 2001, over twenty years had passed since I had first taken to the woods for lengthy and strenuous adventures. Over those years I did camp with my family each summer on vacations to state parks, but those relaxing times, with the conveniences of civilization close at hand, didn't immerse me in the wilderness or test my endurance. Now, with all my children either in college or on their own, I spent long, challenging times on the trail. I trekked along without Meryl's company since she didn't find as much to like in pushing one's body to its limits.

My excursions started with day hikes of eight to ten miles, but in a few years I was hiking almost twenty miles a day with a full backpack and staying out days at a time. At the end of a long day of hiking, after eating some nourishing but less-than-delicious rehydrated fare, I would sit back, relax, and enjoy the tired-but-satisfied feeling that a day of hiking afforded me.

Sometimes I would camp alone, but more often I would make camp along with fellow hikers and enjoy the camaraderie. A type of instant friendship and acceptance forms among those who travel hiking trails. Around a campfire stories flow, especially hiking stories, but any topic could entertain us.

One evening on the Tuscarora Trail, which passes within twenty miles of my home, I reached camp in the evening, having started Friday after work. Two other hikers arrived before me and already had a fire blazing. We exchanged the usual pleasantries about when and where our hike began and what our plans for the next day were while preparing and eating our meals. As the sunlight faded and the darkness of the surrounding woods engulfed us, we sat around the fire enjoying a cool breeze and the opportunity to engage in conversation.

"So you are from these parts, Nimble?" The one who called himself Raven reaffirmed what I had told him earlier, addressing me by my trail name, an appellation I earned from fellow hikers for my penchant of scrambling around huge rock formations at every opportunity. Raven was much younger than me and had jet black, close-cropped hair. His dark, probing eyes and intense presence fit his trail moniker.

"Born and raised," I said.

"Did you follow the Dover trial last fall?"

"Some. Did you?" The 2005 trial over teaching Intelligent Design in Dover, a town about an hour away, brought the topic of evolution into the national spotlight.

"Yeah, I'm a high school biology teacher in the suburbs of Columbus, Ohio."

I nodded. I met people from all over the world on the trail—Europe, Asia, Australia. It tended to be an educated group.

"What did you think of the verdict?" Raven asked.

Before I could muster an answer, the other hiker, Catfish, spoke in a slow drawl. "I didn't think much of it." The man with the bushy brown beard had been rather quiet until then. He kept his soft eyes focused on the fire even as he spoke.

"You think that Intelligent Design is correct?" Raven asked, a bit astonished.

"Well, I think we should keep an open mind. The theory of evolution, as generally accepted, does not have good answers to the questions Behe proposed in his book, *Darwin's Black Box*."

Raven glanced over at Catfish who still gazed at the fire. "Oh, you teach biology, too?" He posed the question in a way that presupposed a "no" answer.

"No, but I followed the issues at the trial."

"Most biologists think they have good answers to Behe's questions."

"Yeah, I know," Catfish replied, "but the answers are not conclusive. Biologists have never shown how molecular systems arose, they've only hinted at the mechanisms that might be responsible. That's a lot different than the theories in physics that have formulas that can be tested."

"True, but the Intelligent Design community hasn't come up with an alternative, other than to invoke a designer with no clues as to how the designer accomplished his work."

The opposing sides of the conversation mirrored a growing struggle within myself. In school I'd always felt that evolution through random genetic mutation and natural selection, or survival of the fittest, made sense, but when I thought of evolution in the context of astral travel and reincarnation, something was missing. In the past several years the question about how the ability for astral travel evolved had plagued me. There couldn't be a gene for an astral body, could there? How could an astral body have survival advantages? If the astral body did not evolve through natural selection, how did it come about? What was the strength of the argument for Intelligent Design? What was its weakness?

In search of answers to these questions I read pro-evolution/anti-Intelligent Design classics like Dawkins's *The Blind Watchmaker* and Dennett's *Darwin's Dangerous Idea,* as well as works from leading proponents of Intelligent Design, including Behe's *Darwin's Black Box* and Dembski's *The Design Inference: Eliminating Chance through Small Probabilities.*

"I agree with what Catfish is saying," I said. "Evolution does not have the weight of theories in science where formulas back up the theory."

"But that doesn't make it wrong," Raven argued.

"Certainly not," I agreed.

Raven grabbed the few remaining twigs lying to his side and threw them into the dying fire. "At least Darwinian evolution has an excellent idea for a mechanism, even if it can't point to a definitive route for evolution. The Intelligent Design advocates just point to a designer, and even Behe has called that designer God. The judge in the trial recognized that and concluded, rightfully I think, that Intelligent Design was just religion in disguise."

I nodded, then picked up a stick to poke at the fire which had died down to embers.

Catfish joined back into the conversation. "Behe's connection to religion sure didn't help his cause."

Raven got up. "I'm gonna see if I can't round up some more firewood," he said as he walked into the brush.

I prodded the smoldering logs some more, trying to encourage a flame, while thinking about why academics found the Intelligent Design argument unconvincing.

"You know, Catfish," I said after giving up on trying to get a flame going, "according to Kuhn, a reigning paradigm is not abandoned until an acceptable replacement takes over."

"Well, I find Intelligent Design acceptable," Catfish mused.

Raven appeared from the brush with a dead branch under each arm. He threw them down beside the fire and then picked one of them up, using his hands and feet to break it into smaller pieces.

As he broke the dead wood he spoke. "You might find Intelligent Design acceptable, but the academic world doesn't."

Catfish shrugged, got up, and stretched a bit before starting to break up the other branch that Raven had dragged into camp.

"I think you're right, Raven," I said. "The academic world is happy with the theory of evolution the way it is. They aren't looking for a replacement."

Raven threw some new pieces of wood on the fire and began to blow on the embers.

"But I have been..."

I watched as new flames leaped into the air as the new pieces caught.

"...and I think I might have one."

Raven threw his last piece on the fire and sat back down. "You've found a replacement to evolution? And it's not called Intelligent Design?"

"Oh, I think that most biologists will still give it that label."

Raven laughed, "Okay, so what is it?"

"Some of the ideas that grabbed me come from Stuart Kauffman and Michael Denton. They have slightly different ways of approaching the concept, but both believe in something some call emergence."

"Emergence?" Catfish had a puzzled look.

"Yes, it's the idea that the self-organizing ability of complex systems has the potential to explain the unique properties of biological systems."

Raven shook his head. "I read some of that, but it begs the question of the mechanism. It still all goes back to a designer."

"Yes and no," I said. "Ultimately everything goes back to a designer, if you accept the Big Bang theory."

"But physicists claim that—"

"I know," I interrupted. "I know about all of those theories that say how God isn't necessary for the Big Bang, but we're here and the laws of the universe have a design in the sense that they exist and make sense."

Raven smiled. "Okay. I agree that the universe has a design. Maybe no designer, though."

"Fair enough," I agreed. "So, why do electrons form around the nucleus of an atom only in certain numbers in particular bands or shells? You know, two electrons in 1s, two in 2s, six in 2p and so forth."

"I don't know. That's just the way that physicists have observed it."

"Why don't some atoms have three electrons in the 1s shell and eight in the 2p shell? Or why isn't there a 2z ring?"

"I have no idea. That's just the way things are."

"Exactly," I said. "Nature has a built-in pattern that dictates how electrons must form around a nucleus. So the argument Denton puts forth has a similar basis, but on a biological level. He is saying that at the macromolecular and subcellular level, physics determines shape or form. He sees the development of a 'law of forms'—that the subcellular forms and properties of living systems arise from the intrinsic nature of matter, just like the way elements are formed through specific numbers of electrons in certain shells."

Raven paused for a moment, then said, "Proteins do have unique forms..." His voice trailed off. After a few seconds he continued. "But I can't see how that explains all the things that natural selection explains."

"Not by itself," I said. "You still have natural selection that works in pruning out the least fit, but the concept of natural forms solves the problem of irreducible complexity arising from random mutations of genes."

"Huh?"

"The argument against Darwinian evolution has always been that the complexity of life forms could not come from random chance. Darwin didn't know about the complexity of cellular biology when he came up with his theory. The position of Denton is that the complex structures necessary for life are part of nature."

Raven shook his head. "Still needs a lot of work." He reached for another stick and tossed it on the fire.

"Oh, for sure," I said as I stood up and stretched, "but I see it as a start."

After a brief moment Raven pointed to the guitar-shaped bag strapped to the side of my backpack. "What's that you got?"

"My backpack guitar," I said.

"How about a few tunes?"

"Yeah, we're gettin' too serious here."

I unpacked my instrument and adjusted the tuning. Before long the topic of evolution became an afterthought as music filled the night.

# Chapter 45

*December 2008, Harrisburg, PA*

After working as a database administrator for a couple of years, I found a more prestigious position as the Director of Research for a large healthcare organization. The nice title, comfy office, and good salary made life simple. My children were all successful on their own. My marriage was stronger than ever going into its thirty-sixth year. Life was good.

My trouble-free existence helped me forget about the work that had gripped me for over two decades. Our country's continued engagement in war against Islamic extremists also kept me feeling distant from the names of Allah. I became apathetic to my system of using the names for emotional stability. With my life running smoothly, I didn't need help to achieve emotional steadiness.

When my family physician felt a bump on my prostate during my physical in November of 2008, he told me to get a biopsy. A quick search online told me that such lumps turned out to be cancerous about fifty percent of the time. I figured that mine would surely be in the benign fifty percent since I always ate copious amounts of fruits and vegetables and exercised daily.

A week after the biopsy I sat in the urologist's exam room expecting to hear that I had gone through the painful biopsy procedure for nothing.

The doctor entered with his clipboard, shut the door, and sat down in the chair beside me.

"You have prostate cancer."

I was not prepared for this pronouncement. It knocked me off balance and sent my comfortable life into a tumble. What were my options? The doctor discussed them with me: surgery, radiation, watchful waiting. Did I want to get rid of the cancer and endure the side effects, or wait and see if it wouldn't get any worse?

A diagnosis of cancer makes one anxious and uncertain about the future. My relative indifference to the names of Allah evaporated.

When the cancer churned my emotions I turned to my Holistic Emotive Practices again and found refuge. I found the best way for me to deal with my anxiety was to take a few minutes, several times a day, to engage in these practices.

Whenever my emotional turbulence tugged at me during work, I got up and closed the office door. I sat on a chair away from my desk and focused on my feelings. I didn't vocalize anything, but instead I sub-articulated, breathed, and thought through a soothing word, allowing it to improve my troubled state.

One name, Muqeet, served me particularly well during this rough period. When I first closed my eyes to search my feelings it usually felt good. It felt like *"mmm,"* this is the right thing to do.

But that *"mmm"* sensation didn't last. I slipped into an uncomfortable realization of my travails, an *"uuh"* feeling.

At that point I just let go of wanting to be in control. The *"q"* helped to let go. The *"q"* didn't work with the preceding *"uuh"* or by itself. Rather, it connected with an *"eee"* which cleared my mind. The *"qee"* together worked to rid all intervening thoughts.

The finishing *"t"* helped establish a feeling of releasing control of my emotions. My rampant negative thoughts of cancer were diminished a little each time I went through the thought processes attending to this word. I would repeat the name several times, restarting the process with each breath. As I breathed in I felt a pleasant feeling. Then, if negative thoughts still persisted, I would feel the *"uuh"* and exorcise those pessimistic concerns as I exhaled *"qeet."*

If a new breath brought a pleasant feeling that wasn't followed by a discouraging thought, but instead a feeling of relaxation, then I deemed my session successful. I would complete this *"maa"* inhalation with an exhale of *"teen,"* expressing in feelings Mateen, another name of Allah. The *"t"* again released control and the *"een"* an exclamation point on the feeling that my emotions now stood in good favor.

The power of the names of Allah to keep my emotions on an even keel rekindled my desire to share my system of using sounds for emotional well-being. Once again I wanted to publish my book on Holistic Emotive Practices. I made some revisions based on my successful use of the names of Allah in dealing with emotional turmoil and felt a need to get feedback.

I gave a draft of my book to my hiking buddy, Steve. Steve and I started hiking together shortly after the collapse of the World Trade

Center towers. We spent about two weeks every year since then on the Appalachian Trail and had hiked almost 2,000 miles of the almost 2,200-mile trail. Our adventures together forged a great friendship and I knew he would give me honest criticism.

# CHAPTER 46

*April 2010, Nantahala Wilderness, NC*

The overcast sky kept getting darker. It meant the impending rain would catch us soon, but nevertheless Steve and I kept an optimistic mood, just thankful to be back on the trail again. We were only three hours into a four-day backpack excursion that would mark our completion of the North Carolina section of the Appalachian Trail. After this trip, less than 200 miles of the entire trail remained for us to hike.

"So how did you learn about the names of Allah?" Steve asked.

"In a book called *Toward the One*."

"Was that a book on Islam?" Steve asked as we continued to hike.

"No," I replied. "The author talked about many different religious paths and claimed that they were all moving toward the same goal, 'the One'... in other words, a relationship with God. He was a Sufi, a mystical branch of Islam."

My answer satisfied Steve for a while, but after another hundred yards or so he fired off another question. "So do you think all religions have the same goal?"

Often we walked the trail in silence, simply enjoying the chance to lose ourselves in nature. Perhaps as many times we carried on conversations as we walked. For us, nothing was off limits—politics and religion, taboo in most social situations, we embraced, so I knew Steve was an unabashed Christian apologist.

"Well, I believe that all religions have the goal of understanding and explaining how things came into being and how we should behave here on this earth," I said.

"Seems like a pretty nebulous goal."

"Yeah, the book glosses over the differences because it is trying to be politically correct."

"So you disagree with its premise?"

I didn't answer right away, but took time to think over my response. When I reached a spot where the trail skirted around several huge boulders, I stopped and looked up at the darkening clouds. Toward the west, and not too far now, we could hear thunder.

"I think that Pir Vilayat's goal of bringing all religions together is exemplary, but the differences between religions are significant, especially the major religions."

Steve gazed at the menacing clouds. Another crack of lightning prompted him to say, "We're going to get wet," before returning to the topic at hand. "What differences are you referring to, and what do you call 'major' religions?"

I started walking again. "There are three religions that I consider major."

"Which ones?" Steve asked. "I know Christianity is one, and Islam is another, right?"

"Yes, and Buddhism."

"Not Hinduism? There are Hindu temples all over the world."

"It's hard to consider Hinduism a single entity since there are so many different forms."

"But that's true in Christianity, too. Protestants versus Catholics, and in Islam, Shiites versus Sunni."

"But their differences are small in comparison to the Hindu sects. All Christians believe in Christ and his resurrection and what it meant for salvation. All Muslims believe that Muhammad was the prophet of God who brought the word of God in the Qur'an. Yet the way a Hindu worships varies from village to village, and even within village based on social class and gender.

"Besides, the Hindu temples outside of India are built almost exclusively by people descended from the Indian subcontinent, or they are a small minority of the surrounding culture," I told him. "Christianity, Islam, and Buddhism have replaced the prevailing religion of a culture in the past millennium. Hinduism hasn't done that for almost two thousand years. Two thousand years ago Hinduism was maybe *the* major world religion, but its claim to that status is not merited today."

"Okay, so how do your three major religions differ?"

I glanced overhead at the ever darkening sky and picked up the pace. We still had a long way to go to reach the shelter. The more we traveled with a dry path the better. I raised my voice as Steve got further behind me. "I think each one focuses primarily on only one part of the human condition."

"What do you mean?" Steve hurried to close the gap between us.

"We, as humans, live in three realms. We live in the physical world where we have to provide for our well being—our food and shelter. We also live in an emotional or social realm with the other people that we come in contact with, especially our families, but really everyone. Finally, our lives have a mental component, an internal dimension of thoughts. These components parallel the three emotional components I wrote about in my book. The physical world with the arousal dimension, the emotional/social with pleasure, and mental with control."

As we continued, the trail started down a steep descent. We had to slow down and watch our footing as we encountered loose rocks. When it leveled off Steve picked up the thread.

"But don't all religions deal with all three human realms? They all prescribe ways to behave to attain salvation, or nirvana, or whatever they choose to call their goal that involve physical, emotional, and mental aspects."

"True. I can't argue with that," I said. "But each emphasizes one of these areas over the other, at least from the way I read it."

"So which religion focuses on which realm?"

"Islam focuses on the physical more than Christianity or Buddhism. Sharia law prescribes much of daily life's activities, and four of its five so-called pillars require some kind of physical act: prayer, fasting, giving alms, and a trip to Mecca. In contrast, Christianity and Buddhism have only general rules of behavior.

"Also, the Qur'an, Islam's holy book, tells the faithful that they must be willing to fight and die in defending Islam against infidels who would try to destroy their faith. Christ tells followers to turn the other check, and the Buddha prohibits killing of any living animal or even dealing in the sale of guns."

I thought about the implications of what I had just said and then added, "That's not to say that I view Islam as a violent religion."

"Certain elements within Islam are," Steve pointed out.

"Agreed. But it would be a mistake to see the extremists as the whole of Islam. I think Islam is simply echoing the true nature of man in the physical realm. We humans have an instinct to defend what we perceive to be ours, and Islam reflects that. I mean, you didn't see our supposed Christian nation turn the other cheek after 9/11, did you?"

"No. You're right."

The lightning was now much closer. We walked in silence for a couple of minutes before Steve came back to the topic. "What about the emotional and mental realms?"

"Paul, in his first letter to the Corinthians, tells you which one Christians should hold as the highest. 'And now these three remain: faith, hope and love'."

"'But the greatest of these is love'," Steve concluded the familiar scripture.

"Right. To Christianity, love—the emotional aspect of man—is the most important human realm. Faith deals with the mental. Hope concerns the future and what will happen. I consider that an attachment to form of some kind. Some might argue non-physical, but nevertheless a form, which to me indicates physical rather than emotional. Love is the emotional aspect."

"Makes sense," Steve agreed.

"Buddhism stands alone on the mental realm. The main precepts of Buddhism, the 'Noble Eightfold Path', include four steps that involve mental concepts—'Right View', 'Right Intention', 'Right Mindfulness', and 'Right Concentration'. In Buddhism the physical and emotional realms are just the source of attachments that cause suffering."

After I laid out this rationale the rain started, gently at first. We stopped to take off our packs and scramble into our rain gear as fast as we could. By the time we had our packs back on we found ourselves in a downpour.

We hiked in steady rain for the remainder of the day's journey, speaking only about the logistics of the trail. Finally, after almost five hours of walking in the rain, we reached a shelter. Crews of volunteer workers from local hiking clubs have constructed them at intervals varying from six to twelve miles. The stuctures are typically three-sided with a wooden platform for sleeping. Some have two or even three sleeping levels, others only a single one. At most shelters you will find a picnic table located just outside.

When we arrived at 3:30 in the afternoon we found an empty structure. It featured a single level with enough room for six persons to sleep comfortably, but one rare feature of the shelter proved useful in the rain. The roof extended out over the picnic table, and a long bench ran along the far side of the area covered by the extension.

We took off our packs and changed into dry clothes. After we laid out our sleeping bags to reserve our space, we sat down on the bench as rain pelted the tin roof above us and looked out into the dripping wet woods from which we had just escaped. The shelter sat nestled in a low area, surrounded by a thick copse of trees that added to the secure feeling the structure itself afforded. Now relaxed, Steve turned back to the topic of religion that the rain had interrupted.

"I know that your beliefs are different than mine. You go to a Christian church, but your tendency toward post-modern philosophy sets you apart."

"I admit that I'm a rarity. My objections to literal interpretations of the Bible don't fit what most of my fellow Christians believe. My convictions make me an atheist, according to Dan Dennett." I laughed at this reflection.

"Dan Dennett? Who's that? Someone who goes to your church?"

I laughed again, this time harder. "No, no. He's a professor at Tufts where I went to grad school. He's a well known philosopher and ardent atheist. In one of his books, *Breaking the Spell*, he says that if you don't pray to a being you consider to be an appropriate recipient of gratitude, then you are an atheist. But I see that as a term used by hardcore materialists who don't believe in a higher level of consciousness than man. I do believe in such consciousness, but I don't see it as a person of any kind."

"But man is made in God's image," Steve protested.

"An image is not the same as the reality."

"Then what is God to you, if not like a person of some sort?"

"Two ideas dance around that question for me. One is called biocentrism, and the other is known as the Cognitive Theoretic Model of the Universe." As I spoke, the torrents of rain beat even louder on the tin roof.

Steve raised his voice over the din. "What? Biocentrism? Is that some kind of humanism?"

I shouted to be heard. "No. Biocentrism states that life and consciousness are essential in explaining the universe."

"Oh, some kind of New Age philosophy."

"No. Robert Lanza would dispute that. He bases his concept of biocentrism on mainstream science. It asserts that you can't ignore consciousness in any theory that tries to explain the universe. He arrives at this from work in quantum mechanics."

I got a curious stare from Steve. "And how does that explain God?"

"Well, we're not there yet. I need the other approach, the Cognitive Theoretic Model of the Universe, or CTMU for short. It was developed by Chris Langan."

"How does a theory of the universe explain God?" Steve asked, not hiding his disbelief.

I thought for a moment and took a sip from my water bottle. The rain abated somewhat and I continued in a more normal voice. "The basis of the CTMU is that any theory of the universe has to consider the observer, just like biocentrism. The CTMU takes it a step further and holds that reality, or the universe as we know it, self-configures and self-processes. It's a form of Intelligent Design theory in a way, but it does not invoke a God as the designer."

"If God isn't the designer, then who is? Obviously man can't be."

"There is no who. The design is a process. It leaves the position open to the participants in the universe. In other words, intelligent beings that inhabit it, which would include us, but not necessarily the physical portion of us. His ideas come from complexity theory and the science of self-organizing systems. He characterizes the universe as participatory. Kind of like the collective consciousness designs it as we develop."

Steve shook his head. "You lost me there."

I held up the palms of my hands in a gesture of helplessness. I didn't try to get any further into the obtuse ideas.

"So how do you reconcile those beliefs with your status in the Christian church?"

"I'm comfortable following the moral teachings of Christ."

Steve seemed less than satisfied with my non-answer, but didn't comment. We both sat listening to the rain on the tin for a while. After a minute or so I spoke again.

"I don't think it is a coincidence that we have three major religions. My Christian beliefs are for my emotional realm, which I feel is the most important. The names of Allah fit into my physical realm. We can't ignore our existence in the physical world. I find it beneficial to study what the prophet Muhammad has said. As far as the mental realm, I think that the Buddha got it right on that level. Gurdjieff would say that there are three major religions because of the Law of Three."

"Gurdjieff? The Law of Three?" A gust of wind blew rain in the side of the shelter, spraying us. We got up from our seat on the bench.

"Did you ever see a picture of a fractal?" I asked after sitting down on the picnic table, which had remained dry.

"Yes, you mean those pictures where the pattern is repeated as you keep getting deeper and deeper into the image?"

"Right. Well, that kind of pattern repetition fits with the saying 'as above, so below'. You can see the pattern of physical, emotional, and mental in the superstructure of human beliefs through the three major religions. The pattern repeats in the makeup of human physiology, and in human behavior, and human speech sounds. You also see a pattern of three in other areas, like laws of physics, where there are gravity, nuclear forces, and electromagnetic forces."

As I finished my statement we saw four hikers approaching the shelter through the rain. I had a question for Steve that I wanted to ask before the others joined us.

"What did you think of the ideas I presented in the book? I mean the connections of emotions to sounds."

"Well, to be honest, it was rather dry. I did read it all, but it wasn't easy."

"I know," I sighed. I had written it in an academic fashion with loads of references and technical jargon. "There's a lot of information to convey."

"Couldn't you find some way to interject a personal twist to the story? Like how you came upon the different discoveries? I think that would make it more readable. I mean, if you want to reach a larger audience, that's what you're going to need to do."

The hikers reached the shelter and took off their wet gear in the confusion of many bodies in a small space. Rain gear and packs hung throughout the shelter. We heated pots of water on small pack stoves and added dehydrated meals. Trail stories, tunes on backpack guitars, and laughter all filled the dry enclave as a pouring rain beat on the roof.

# CHAPTER 47

*November 2010, New Cumberland, PA*

After Steve advised me to add a personal twist to my story, I needed to make a decision. Could I write about my experiences with astral travel and reincarnation? Since I hadn't held an academic position for a decade, the risk of humiliation from that realm no longer inhibited me. The vast majority of people believe that science cannot explain away the mysteries that get labeled as spiritual or paranormal. It was those people I decided to target.

In the process of recording the events of my life, I researched what others had written or recorded on the supernatural or paranormal. The number of sources was staggering. Finding material was no problem, but limiting the amount that I amassed was. In my online searches for interesting ideas I noticed the Spirit Society of Pennsylvania's website indicating monthly meetings at a location near us. I saw a chance to interact with others on the topic instead of just reading or listening.

Meryl and I attended a meeting and I got a chance to talk with the leader of the group, Kelly Weaver, a psychic-medium who did intuitive readings and past life regressions for people. My only other experience with a psychic was Ruth Este—serious, all business, quite dour. Kelly was none of these. She was a vivacious, attractive, middle-aged woman who spoke in a light-hearted manner and laughed a great deal.

"We like to give new people a chance to tell everyone a little bit about themselves—why they are interested in the Spirit Society. Maybe you could relate any experiences you've had with supernatural events," Kelly told us upon our arrival.

"How much time are we allowed?" I grinned. "I could talk all night."

Kelly's eyes lit up. "Oh, really?"

I gave an abbreviated account of my experiences and research centered on the phenomena of spirit bodies. By the end of our conversation she asked if I would give a presentation at an upcoming meeting. I accepted the invitation.

## *January 2011, New Cumberland, PA*

The night of my talk, about two dozen persons showed up. Meryl's presence added a special dimension for me. Her indifference to my efforts aimed at connecting spiritual pursuits to rational, scientific investigation had been thawing ever since our youngest left for college. Our competitiveness diminished and we were again finding common ground. That, along with the informal atmosphere and the nature of the group, put me at ease. How hard could it be to talk about spirit bodies to a group whose stated purpose was to investigate disembodied spirits? The forty-minute talk went well. Afterwards, a young woman with short, curly, dark hair and penetrating brown eyes introduced herself as Leslie.

"So you are one of those Ph.D.s who actually believes in spirits?" Leslie's tone registered mock disbelief.

"Yes," I said, while putting my laptop in its case. "They don't really make you take an oath not to believe in spirits before they give you your diploma."

She laughed. "Right, but it's frustrating to me that the scientific world is so vehemently against anything spiritual."

As I stuffed the cords to my LCD projector in the case I looked up and nodded. "I know. A majority of scientists use unconscious matter as the starting point for all theories about the universe, rather than consciousness. Matter before mind." I zipped the case of the projector. "However, I see more and more people in the scientific community acknowledging consciousness as a fundamental aspect of nature, and basic to any theory explaining the universe." These scientists see consciousness as something more than a phenomenon generated through complex neurological circuitry. The complexity of our brains allows us to do much with our consciousness, but consciousness came first. In other words, mind before matter."

I picked up my laptop bag and projector case. "Do you want to grab some refreshments?" I asked and pointed to the back of the room where my wife and others stood around two tables of food.

After helping ourselves to snacks, our conversation continued. "I understand the frustration with the scientific community," I said. "When scientists who study paranormal activity answer one objection from a skeptic, the skeptic always comes up with another. Take ESP, for example. Critics claim the results are due to something other than ESP, even though they can't point to any flaws in the experiment."

"I know," Leslie said. "When people report information about a past reincarnation or something seen via astral travel during near death experiences it's the same thing. Skeptics claim that they must have gotten the information in some other way, even when no other plausible explanation exists in many, many cases."

"Of course the skeptics will disagree with that assessment," I said with a laugh.

Leslie smiled. "Always."

"I, too, was once skeptical, even after I experienced astral travel, even though I couldn't see how my mind could fabricate the experience. And all of the events in my life that pointed to reincarnation... I chalked up to coincidence, a really, really highly improbable coincidence, but coincidence, nonetheless."

Leslie looked surprised. "So how did you overcome your skepticism?"

"A premonition."

"What do you mean? You just had an intuitive feeling that your experiences were real?"

"No. One day, a few years back, I was working in the yard. My wife came out and told me that she was going to drive out to her folks' place. When she opened the door to get in the car, I saw the front of the vehicle, just in front of the driver's side front wheel, take on a crumpled look, like it had been in an accident.

"This puzzled me. After a couple of seconds the vision disappeared, and I told my wife that I'd join her later.

"When I arrived at my in-laws thirty minutes later, I found that my wife had been in a minor accident. The dent in the car from the wreck perfectly matched my earlier vision. Now, a skeptic might tell me that I didn't remember the sequence correctly, or that I was fabricating all or part of the story, in order to keep his or her skeptical world order intact. That's fine for the skeptic. I don't expect my experience to change someone else's basic beliefs. But I know what I saw and when I saw it.

"If you can have perceptions of this nature, which reductionist science can't explain, then it is not such a jump to believe that we have spirit bodies."

Others had joined around our discussion. A few related personal experiences, including one man who had a near-death experience. I spoke with people of various backgrounds, including a lawyer and someone with a master's degree in social work. Everyone was quite engaging and nobody skeptical. To that crowd, the paranormal was normal.

On our way home Meryl asked, "Are you glad you came?"

"Yes, I'm finally telling people about my astral travel and reincarnation. It's therapeutic."

# CHAPTER 48

*August 2011, Rural Central ME*

The portion of the Appalachian Trail in Maine affords the enterprising hiker some opportunities not present on the rest of the trail. At 115 miles from the northern terminus of the trail the Hundred-Mile Wilderness begins. For 100 miles you encounter no civilization, save for a couple of logging roads traveled only by huge logging trucks and occasional foolhardy persons with four-wheel-drive vehicles. If one successfully negotiates the rough, rocky trail through and around the lakes, ponds, and bogs, the final task remains—the ascent up Mt. Katahdin, the longest continuous climb on the entire trail—a fitting end to my almost ten-year quest to hike the entire Appalachian Trail.

Steve and I started in late August at Monson, the jumping off point at the southern end of the 100-mile trek. We left with full packs, anxious to be back in the woods again. I felt strong, cancer-free for over two years, having rid myself of the tumors through surgery a few months after the diagnosis. We both were excited by the challenge ahead. The most we had ever hiked without stopping for resupply was five days and seventy miles through the Smokey Mountains.

On the fifth day into the anticipated seven-day hike we stopped for lunch by one of the many ponds that dot the trail in this section of Maine. I could no longer keep silent. "So did you get a chance to read the updated manuscript I sent you?"

"Yes, I found it much more readable overall," Steve said between bites of his power bar. "But there were a few things I found hard to comprehend... Like when you talked about reincarnation, and the part about the guys you encountered after that bike ride."

"You don't comprehend it? Or you don't believe it?"

"Well, with the reincarnation stuff, I'm not a believer, and your alleged encounter with Castaneda seemed too much like name dropping or just plain fantasy."

I shook my head again. "Believe me, I know how it sounds." I was silent for over a minute, thinking back on the encounter. "I know skeptics will have a field day. Since I was once committed to a hospital for psychiatric reasons, my sanity will be forever questioned. They won't consider the circumstances that led up to the affair. Do you think I was delusional?"

"You've always been one of the most together persons I've known... and one of the most honest. It's just that it was so unusual."

"I revered Castaneda's ideas in my twenties, before I encountered Gurdjieff's work. And the weird thing is that it appears that Castaneda got some of his ideas from Gurdjieff, according to a book by William Patterson. It's pretty fascinating. If Castaneda was connected to the ideas of Gurdjieff, and Gurdjieff's reincarnation held Castaneda's work in high esteem..." I paused for a moment.

"The intellectual efforts of those two captivated millions of minds this past century. Not mainstream academics, but everyday people who seek practical ways to learn the truth in an organic fashion that applies to their lives." I stood up and stared across the pond. The mirror reflection of the blue sky and clouds in the pond made the far shore appear as though it floated in the air. "It was karma that led to the encounter. It was just a process I had to go through."

I realized that I used the argument of reincarnation, a phenomenon that Steve didn't buy, to explain something that he couldn't comprehend. It was destined to be a futile effort.

"Well, right now our karma is to keep hiking these hundred miles of wilderness so we can climb Katahdin." Steve got up and put on his pack. "Come on, a mountain awaits us."

I put on my pack and followed.

This stretch of trail passes several isolated mountain lakes, welcome refreshment to a sweaty hiker. When we arrived at a beach along the shores of Nahmakanta Lake, we wasted no time in shedding our packs and stripping to our skivvies to take a plunge in the cool, clear water.

We floated on our backs in total relaxation until Steve asked, "How do you reconcile reincarnation with evolution?"

I stopped floating and stood up.

"If you believe in evolution," he asked, "how did we get the reincarnation gene?"

"Devotees of Darwin would find the concept of reincarnation laughable," I said. "How could natural selection account for something that has no apparent survival value for the organism? But I am not wed to Darwinism as the be-all and end-all of human development.

"Stuart Kauffman and others argue that self-organization in complex systems may play a more important role in evolution than natural selection. They make a case that new traits emerge as complex biological processes self-organize, from a more or less random state to an ordered one, spontaneously. He doesn't point to a specific force in nature that accounts for this ability to self-organize, but others have.

"Ilya Prigogine says the effect of gravity increases with the complexity of the system. The brain has often been called the most complex system known. Can the gravitational forces of the sun or galaxy somehow coalesce an energy field associated with a person into a cohesive form? And then can that form—the energy field of a person that some might call the astral body—survive the death of the physical body? Maybe our ability to reincarnate comes about through this process in an emergent manner."

Steve pondered this before standing and looking over the lake to the opposite shore. "Yeah, it's an interesting theory, I guess, but no way can it be proven." He splashed water with both hands then turned to wade toward the shore.

I followed him. My body temperature had lowered enough that the water felt too cold. "You can show evidence that supports a theory or you can disprove it, but never fully prove its validity. I believe that my story supports the theory."

We headed toward the rocks where we'd left our boots and clothes. "I don't know," Steve said as he sat on a rock. "Even if I could accept your theory for reincarnation, making a claim to be the reincarnation of some famous person seems like a cheap bid for fame."

I picked up my boots and sat near him. "I'm not trying to further Gurdjieff's teachings or get persons who follow his work to pay homage to me. That would be absurd. I'm not trying to stand on his shoulders. I want my work with sounds and emotions to stand on its own. It has nothing to do with Gurdjieff."

I laced up my boots.

"There are only two reasons I present the Gurdjieff stuff. First, it helps to explain how my ideas developed, and second, I think it contributes to a greater understanding of human nature."

"Reincarnation helps us understand human nature?"

"Yes, by showing that we have higher bodies. When the physical body is gone, something survives."

"Higher bodies?"

I stood up. "That's another conversation," I said. "Let's hike."

We put on our packs and started back on the trail.

We reached our day's destination around five in the afternoon. We had traveled eighteen miles over rough terrain, but since we didn't have to climb any sizable mountains and our packs had only a couple of days of food left, it seemed like an easy day compared to the first four.

Soon after we reached the tenting area another hiker arrived. "Deacon," as he called himself, had been on the trail almost six months, all the way from Georgia. He stood 6'4" and had a big, red, bushy beard, a real bear of a man. We always enjoyed the company of thru-hikers—those who hike the whole trail in one long trip—because of the great stories they invariably tell. The three of us pitched our tents and made our evening meals.

After I finished eating I scouted for firewood, but found next to none. The high volume of traffic, even on this remote stretch of trail, often meant walking quite a distance to find dead wood to burn. I resigned myself to a night without a fire and sat down with my guitar on a log next to the fire pit and played some music.

Steve and Deacon soon joined me.

One common hiker ritual is to inquire about the origin of trail names. "Where does 'Deacon' come from?" Steve asked our fellow hiker after I finished playing a tune.

"Somebody 'bout five months ago said I looked like a deacon and it stuck. I guess it has something to do with my size and my serious look."

"So we're not going to get a sermon, then?" I joked.

Deacon laughed. "Not from me."

"Well, I already had my sermon today, thank you." Steve cracked a smile.

"Oh, yeah?" Deacon asked. "Who's been preaching to you?"

"Nimble here has been filling my ear about reincarnation."

"That reminds me," I turned to Steve. "You sounded puzzled at the lake when I said one of the reasons I included reincarnation in the book was to show that we have higher bodies. Remember?"

Steve's face looked blank for a moment before he replied, "Oh, yeah. Higher bodies. I wasn't sure what you meant." Then he turned to Deacon and said, "He's written a book."

"In the process," I said. "I wrote about how different gravitational systems can account for the astral body and the mental body. Don't you remember?" I asked Steve.

"Uh, I can't recall it exactly."

I put my guitar down, got up, and walked the short distance to my pack. I opened the lower flap and retrieved a stack of papers. "Here. I wasn't sure I would show you this, but take a look." I handed the papers to Steve.

"What is it?"

"It's a copy of the talk I recently gave at the Spirit Society of Pennsylvania."

"Were you at a séance or something?"

"Hardly. The society meets monthly to discuss paranormal topics."

"*Spirit Bodies and Beyond*," Steve read the title.

I felt an urge to disappear into the woods as he examined the papers and began to read. I still had ambiguous feelings about showing others what I had written. I believed in what I wrote, but I knew that many would not because they had not experienced what I had. This uneasy feeling prompted an idea for a temporary escape.

"My turn to get water," I said. "Give me your water containers."

I collected Steve's and Deacon's water bottles and bladders, put on my headlamp, and headed down the blue-blazed path marked "water." The Appalachian Trail in Maine has abundant water sources, but sometimes you have to walk a bit from the campsite. After a tenth of a mile down a rocky trail filled with tree roots, a small stream emptied into a lake. Once there, I lined up the six containers on a flat rock, hooked up the plastic hoses to my filter, and pumped.

I took my time in the dimming light, enjoying the sense of oneness with the wilderness. While I stood in the twilight I heard the first loon call of the evening. Its haunting sound echoed across the lake and filled the stillness with an enchanting quality. When I finished pumping, I put my filter away and collected the bottles. Then I sat down on a rock rather than hurrying back to camp.

While I listened to the loons calling, I thought about my life's experiences and the paper I just handed to Steve. I made a commitment when I spoke at the Spirit Society meeting to no longer shy away from my past. I resolved to present my views on man's nature and not worry about detractors. It was easy with the Spirit Society, where everyone shared a belief in a separate spirit, but now I had taken a step and let others see my thoughts.

After sitting and soaking in the evening, pondering my chosen path for about fifteen minutes, I took a deep breath, gathered the water containers, and headed back. With the last rays of light slipping away, the first stars appeared in the clear sky. I needed the light from my headlamp to negotiate the roots and rocks on the path.

When I reached camp I distributed the water and sat again on the log beside Deacon, who put down the papers containing my Spirit Society talk.

"What do you think?" I asked.

"Interesting. I read Raymond Moody's work on near-death experiences and some of the reincarnation material before."

"Yeah, there's a lot out there that suggests there is more to humans than a physical body."

"But scientists don't go for spiritual things like that. Materialists see that kind of talk as pure nonsense," Deacon said.

"I know the general consensus of the academic world, but I believe that higher bodies are materialistic."

Steve, who had been rearranging items in his pack, rejoined us around the non-existent fire.

"Aren't you trying to have it both ways?" he asked when he sat down. "How can you claim that spirit bodies are materialistic?"

I turned off my headlamp to keep from shining light in Steve's eyes. He and Deacon turned theirs off, too.

"I believe there is a physical reality behind our higher bodies. They don't just manifest as a dream or a figment of the imagination or in another dimension. You read what I said about gravity?"

"Sure, the moon, the sun and the stars have a gravitational influence at some level, but how can they be responsible for a separate body? It sounds bizarre."

"For most people the bodies remain inseparable. Based on personal experience, I believe you can learn to separate them through certain practices, but most people don't learn how to do that. When the physical body dies, the other bodies shed the empty shell and continue to exist."

"Material bodies?" Deacon voiced his skepticism.

"I use the term 'body' loosely. The nature of the higher bodies differs from the physical body. They don't possess mass. The astral body exists as energy, which can resemble a sort of mirage, I suppose.

"But the mental and other higher bodies probably only exist in the form of ideas and consciousness. They may exist in some form of forcefield associated with gravity, but it's all guesswork based on convincing evidence for reincarnation, personal experience, and the physics that we do know. But in any case, don't think of the mental body as resembling the physical body in a visual sense."

After a few seconds of silence I continued. "Whatever form the higher bodies take, it seems that it's the mental body which reincarnates."

"But the Christian religion doesn't believe in reincarnation," Steve interjected.

"Did you know that twenty-five percent of all Catholics believe in reincarnation," I said, "even though it goes against their teachings? And over twenty percent of Protestants believe in reincarnation, too."

We could hear the faint cry of loons in the distance, and we sat quietly in the dark listening.

"Hey, let's walk down to the lake," I said. "We can hear the loons better down there and see a lot more sky over the lake. The stars should be spectacular."

We turned our headlamps back on. I took the lead since I had already traveled the route. About halfway there I heard Deacon say, "Your material explanation of spirit bodies is intriguing. I gather you think of this as God's great plan? So I guess it rules out evolution."

"I think these spirit bodies emerged as part of our evolution."

"Emerged?"

"Call it Intelligent Design, if you must. Once you understand that consciousness plays an essential role in any representation of the universe—that you can't have any theory of the universe without an observer, a consciousness—then some form of Intelligent Design makes eminent sense.

"As to whether you call this God's plan, I guess that depends on how you define God. I like to characterize the universe as participatory, or self-creating. The self I refer to forms our highest body, our highest sheath. We all share this 'Self'. It connects us to the entire universe and provides the driving force in our evolution. It creates our collective existence."

We walked the rest of the way to the lake in silence. Once there we turned off our lights and sat on rocks, listening to the magical calling of loons under a billion stars.

# Epilogue

About one year after I finished hiking the Appalachian Trail I submitted my book to a publisher and felt overjoyed when I received a "congratulations" letter accepting the work. This came after many, many rejections. My delight proved premature however, as the small independent company went out of business just weeks before my launch date. I mustered my best stoic response and went back to querying literary agents and pitching publishing houses, but I didn't get a single nibble. After several months without success, I stopped trying to generate interest in the world of traditional publishing.

Getting a book in print via self-publishing has become a fairly easy process. I resisted going this route until now for two reasons. My biggest holdup was pride. I didn't want to be seen as taking an ego trip with a vanity press. I have published over a dozen articles in various scientific and literary journals. At one point a company invested time and money into my memoir. If I couldn't get some party to buy into what I had to say, then I didn't see the point of forcing the issue. The other roadblock was fear of the stigma I had often seen associated with self-publishing. Most of that stemmed from the lack of good editing. Although I felt my work had been well-edited, that fact didn't get me past the narrative linked to purchasing authorship. Two things helped me get past these hang-ups and changed my attitude toward going it alone—a Sufi group and a friend.

The internet has in many ways changed the way we socialize—some of these good, some not so much. Meetups.com was established in 2002 in an effort to combat social isolation in our modern fast-paced world. Over the past decade or so I have joined several groups through the Meetups website. The one that made a significant difference in my social life holds gatherings for the purpose of Sufi meditation. From getting to know the leader and attendees of our small gatherings I learned about the Farm of Peace, the site of Sufi School East. The rural campus, located about an hour and a half from my place, holds workshops and retreats that teach Sufi practices to seasoned initiates as well as newcomers. In the summer of 2018 I attended my first conference there.

I found a receptive audience for my work on emotions and sounds with this community. When I discussed the names of Allah from the viewpoint of my work, people perked up. They wanted to explore the ideas in a deeper fashion. This interest reawakened my desire to get my work published. At a seminar in 2019, I discussed this goal with one of the presenters who has written several well-received books. He had gone the self-publishing route and recommended it.

His success prompted me to explore various options available on the internet, but I had reservations about all of them. Who could I trust? Would it be worth the cost? After six months of resistance what finally got me over my reluctance was a friend.

Dianne chairs a committee that oversees a project at the local Unitarian Universalist church which funds secondary education for girls in Mozambique. I'm also on the committee which corresponds in various ways, including emails. When I gave her my email address—*brian@holisticemotivepractices.com*—she wanted to know what constituted Holistic Emotive Practices. I told her about my work and the website that goes along with the email address. The conversation veered into my writings and thwarted efforts to get the work into print. When she related her experience in helping a friend get a book published and enthusiastically endorsed the company she worked with—Year of the Book—I knew I had found the outlet for my memoir.

In addition to this tome I am also releasing a second treatise, one that focuses on my scientific efforts, entitled *Sufi Mindfulness Practices*. For those of you who would like to get an in-depth understanding of how to use speech sounds to effectively modulate your moods, I encourage you to seek out this book.

With the release of these two volumes I am now sharing my experiences and ideas with interested parties and finding peace and satisfaction in a life that has come full circle.

# ACKNOWLEDGMENTS

Writing a memoir didn't really cross my mind when I first began to keep a journal. I put words on paper about strange happenings and my reactions to them simply to stay grounded. After leaving academia I finally decided that I wanted to tell my story. I gathered courage to send early drafts to friends. To these people I owe my gratitude for their insights. Thanks to Jerry Wexler for helping me see the gaps the reader needed filled. Thank you to Terri Bogle for pointing out where I ran too far into the weeds. And thanks also to Norm Therrien for your encouragement in getting me to tell the really hard parts. These folks played a significant role in easing me into the field of publishing.

I have had the pleasure of working with two excellent editors in fine tuning the manuscript. My first editor, Sandy Nork, ensured that I had a complete story. Thank you Sandy for making me feel like an author. Finally, Demi Stevens of Year of the Book used her keen ability to streamline language to give the story more life. I will be forever grateful for your expertise in providing the final polish. And I can't forget Dianne Dusman whose interest and connection to Year of the Book gave me the final impetus to get the book to the public. Thanks, Dianne. I'm fortunate to have you as a friend.

My life's journey would have been much less interesting without the guidance of a number of teachers. I want to thank my first yoga instructor, William Mandel, for urging me to seek inner truth and for playing an integral role in the establishment of SKY Land, the retreat center which holds a dear spot in my heart. I especially want to thank William's teacher, Dr. Vejayandra Pratap, the director of the Yoga Research Society. Thank you, Dr. Pratap, for providing me a role model in using scientific methods to investigate spiritual practices. Your example has inspired and penetrated me deeply.

I have had the opportunity to study with two spiritual leaders whose work with sounds and chanting became my life's most significant influence. I am thankful to Amrit Desai, the founder of Kripalu Yoga, who used his powerful voice to enchant me. And Pir

Vilayat Inayat Khan, may you rest in peace, I am thankful for your words of inspiration concerning Sufi practices.

Finally, I owe so much to my wife and her more than fifty years of love and support. You have been there for me through all my trials. I can't thank you enough.

# BIBLIOGRAPHY

The following books were referenced either directly or obliquely in the text:

Behe, Michael. *Darwin's Black Box: The Biochemical Challenge to Evolution*. New York, NY: Simon & Schuster, 1996.

Behe, Michael. *The Edge of Evolution: The Search for the Limits of Darwinism*. New York, NY: Simon & Schuster, 2007.

Broughton, Richard. *Parapsychology: The Controversial Science*. New York, NY: Random House, 1991.

Castaneda, Carlos. *A Separate Reality*. New York, NY: Simon & Schuster, 1971.

Castaneda, Carlos. *The Eagle's Gift*. New York, NY: Simon & Schuster, 1981.

Castaneda, Carlos. *The Teachings of Don Juan: A Yaqui Way of Knowledge*. Los Angeles, CA: The University of California Press, 1969.

Chalmers, David. *The Conscious Mind: In Search of a Fundamental Theory*. Oxford, UK: Oxford University Press, 1996.

Davies, Paul. *The Goldilocks Enigma: Why is the Universe Just Right for Life?* New York, NY: Houghton Mifflin Company, 2006.

Dawkins, Richard. *The Blind Watchmaker: Why the Evidence of Evolution Reveals a Universe without Design*. New York, NY: W.W. Norton and Company, 1986.

Dembski, William. *The Design Inference: Eliminating Chance through Small Probabilities*. Cambridge, UK: Cambridge University Press, 1998.

Dennett, Daniel. *Breaking the Spell: Religion as a Natural Phenomenon*. New York, NY: Viking, 2006.

Dennett, Daniel. *Darwin's Dangerous Idea: Evolution and the Meaning of Life*. New York, NY: Simon & Schuster, 1995.

Denton, Michael. "An Anti-Darwinian Intellectual Journey" in *Uncommon Dissent: Intellectuals Who Find Darwinism Unconvincing*. Wilmington, DE: ISI Press, 2004.

Fuller, C. J. *The Camphor Flame: Popular Hinduism and Society in India*. Princeton, NJ: Princeton University Press, 1992.

Gershon, Michael. *The Second Brain: The Scientific Basis of Gut Instinct and a Groundbreaking New Understanding of Nervous Disorders of the Stomach and Intestines*. New York, NY: Harper Collins, 1998.

Gleick, James. *Chaos: Making a New Science*. New York, NY: Viking Penguin, Inc., 1987.

Hesse, Herman. *Steppenwolf*. New York, NY: Henry Holt, 1929.

Hesse, Herman. *The Glass Bead Game: (Magister Ludi), A Novel*. New York, NY: Holt, Rinehart, & Winston, 1969.

Horn, Stacy. *Unbelievable: Investigations into Ghosts, Poltergeists, Telepathy, and Other Unseen Phenomena, from the Duke Parapsychology Laboratory*. New York, NY: HarperCollins, 2009.

Huxley, Aldous. *The Doors of Perception*. New York, NY: Harper & Brothers, 1954.

Kauffman, Stuart. *At Home in the Universe: The Search for the Laws of Self-Organization and Complexity*. New York, NY: Oxford University Press, 1995.

Khan, Pir Vilayat Inayat. *Toward the One*. New York, NY: Harper & Row, 1974.

Kuhn, Thomas. *The Structure of Scientific Revolutions*. London, UK: The University of Chicago Press, 1962.

Lanza, Robert & Bob Berman. *Biocentrism: How Life and Consciousness are the Keys to Understanding the True Nature of the Universe*. Dallas, TX: Benbella Books, 2009.

Mailer, Norman. *The Naked and the Dead*. New York, NY: Rinehart and Co., 1948.

Moody, Raymond. *Life After Life: The Investigation of a Phenomenon—Survival of Bodily Death*. New York, NY: Mockingbird Books, 1975.

Newton, Michael. *Journey of Souls: Case Studies of Life Between Lives*. St. Paul, MN: Llewellyn Publications, 2001.

Ouspensky, P. D. *In Search of the Miraculous*. New York, NY: Harcourt Brace Jovanovich, 1949.

Ouspensky, P. D. *The Fourth Way*. New York, NY: Alfred A. Knopf, 1957.

Patterson, William Patrick. *The Life and Teachings of Carlos Castaneda*. Fairfax, CA: Arete Communications, 2008.

Pei, Mario. *The Story of Language*. Philadelphia, PA: J.B. Lippincott, 1949.

Penrose, Roger. *Shadows of the Mind: A Search for the Missing Science of Consciousness*. New York, NY: Oxford University Press, 1994.

Peter, Fritz. *Boyhood with Gurdjieff*. New York, NY: E.P. Sutton, 1964.

Prigogine, Ilya. *Order Out of Chaos: Man's New Dialogue with Nature*. New York, NY: Bantam Books, 1984.

Ram Dass. *Be Here Now*. San Cristobal, NM: Lama Foundation, 1971.

Rama, Swami, Rudolph Ballentine, & Allan Weinstock. *Yoga and Psychotherapy: The Evolution of Consciousness*. Glenview, IL: Himalayan Institute, 1976.

Saraswati, Satyananda. *Asana, Pranayama, Mudra, Bandha*. Mungar, Bihar, India: Yoga Publications Trust, 2008.

Stevenson, Ian. *Children Who Remember Previous Lives: A Question of Reincarnation*. Charlottesville, VA: The University Press of Virginia, 1987.

Suzuki, D. T. *An Introduction to Zen Buddhism*. New York, NY: Grove Press, 1959.

Taimni, I. K. *The Science of Yoga*. Madras, India: The Theosophical Publishing House, 1961.

Tolkien, J. R. R. *Lord of the Rings*. New York, NY: Houghton Mifflin, 1965.

Wallace, Amy. *Sorcerer's Apprentice: My Life with Carlos Castaneda*. Berkeley, CA: Frog, Ltd, 2003.

Weiss, Brian. *Many Lives, Many Masters: The True Story of a Prominent Psychiatrist, His Young Patient, and the Past-Life Therapy that Changed Both Their Lives*. New York, NY: Simon & Schuster, 1988.

Weiss, Brian. *Only Love is Real: A Story of Soulmates Reunited*. New York, NY: Warner Books, 1996.

Wilhelm, Richard & Cary Baynes. *I Ching*. New York, NY: Bollinger Foundation, 1950.

Zajonc, R. B., Sheila T. Murphy & Marita Inglehart. "Feeling and facial efference: Implications of the vascular theory of emotion." *Psychological Review*, vol. 96, no. 3, 1989, pp. 395–416.

www.ingramcontent.com/pod-product-compliance
Lightning Source LLC
LaVergne TN
LVHW041540070426
835507LV00011B/845